P9-DBM-710

ABOUT THE
BETTY FORD CENTER

The Betty Ford Center was dedicated in 1983 in honor of former First Lady Betty Ford. Conceived as the pilot facility under a new California law that licensed chemical dependency recovery hospitals, the center was widely hailed for focusing awareness on the widespread nature of alcoholism and drug dependency in this country.

Well into its second decade, the center has successfully treated thousands of patients who suffer from a broad range of alcohol and drug-abuse illnesses, and remains at the forefront of research and education in this area. Located at the Eisenhower Medical Center in Rancho Mirage, California, the Betty Ford Center also operates a renowned tutorial program in addiction-treatment medicine for medical students, perpetuating a legacy of service to communities nationwide.

For orders other than by individual consumers, Pocket Books grants a discount on the purchase of **10 or more** copies of single titles for special markets or premium use. For further details, please write to the Vice-President of Special Markets, Pocket Books, 1633 Broadway, New York, NY 10019-6785, 8th Floor.

For information on how individual consumers can place orders, please write to Mail Order Department, Simon & Schuster Inc., 200 Old Tappan Road, Old Tappan, NJ 07675.

THE
BETTY FORD
CENTER
BOOK OF ANSWERS

HELP FOR THOSE STRUGGLING
WITH SUBSTANCE ABUSE
AND FOR THE PEOPLE
WHO LOVE THEM

JAMES W. WEST, M.D., F.A.C.S.

PREFACE BY BETTY FORD

POCKET BOOKS
New York   London   Toronto   Sydney   Tokyo   Singapore

The sale of this book without its cover is unauthorized. If you purchased this book without a cover, you should be aware that it was reported to the publisher as "unsold and destroyed." Neither the author nor the publisher has received payment for the sale of this "stripped book."

The ideas, procedures, and suggestions in this book are intended to supplement, not replace, the medical advice of trained professionals. All matters regarding your health require medical supervision. Consult your physician before adopting the medical suggestions in this book as well as about any condition that may require diagnosis or medical attention.

An *Original* Publication of POCKET BOOKS

POCKET BOOKS, a division of Simon & Schuster Inc.
1230 Avenue of the Americas, New York, NY 10020

Copyright © 1997 by Betty Ford Center

All rights reserved, including the right to reproduce this book or portions thereof in any form whatsoever. For information address Pocket Books, 1230 Avenue of the Americas, New York, NY 10020

West, James W.
    The Betty Ford Center book of answers / James W. West ; preface by Betty Ford.
        p.   cm.
    ISBN 0-671-00182-5
    1. Substance abuse—Miscellanea.   2. Substance abuse—Treatment—Miscellanea.   I. Title.
RC564.29.W47   1997
616.86—DC20   96-41485
                                                                CIP

First Pocket Books trade paperback printing February 1997

10   9   8   7   6   5   4   3   2   1

POCKET and colophon are registered trademarks of Simon & Schuster Inc.

Cover design by Lisa Litwack
Cover photo by C. Aurness/Westlight

Printed in the U.S.A.

To my wife,
Shirley J. West

Acknowledgments

Many thanks to John M. Boop
for nurturing the concept of this book,
Billie Fitzpatrick for her editing skills,
Loretta Barrett for her professional support,
Ronald S. Konecky for his technical support, and
John T. Schwarzlose for his encouragement.

CONTENTS

Contents

PREFACE BY MRS. BETTY FORD

Seventeen years ago, as Ambassador Leonard Firestone and I sat in the study of Jerry's and my home, we discussed our dream for a "new kind" of chemical dependency treatment center. Leonard had casually stopped over, as he often does, when we got to talking about the programs both he and I had participated in for our own treatment. And it was from this neighborly visit that the conception of what is now known as the Betty Ford Center began.

We had a dream of a facility that would stand here in our own community—in the desert of Rancho Mirage, California. Together, we envisioned a setting where our patients would enjoy the tranquillity of our mountains and the vastness of our desert. We wanted a center, not a hospital, where those seeking treatment would find a feeling of home away from home. And so the Betty Ford Center was created.

Today, our seven buildings stand in a campuslike setting around a beautiful lake with the magnificent San Jacinto Mountains as a backdrop. Our unique fourteen-and-one-half-acre campus offers a climate of serenity and peace, and an environment that speaks to the dignity of each woman and man who makes the personal decision to enter treatment at the Betty Ford Center.

Here, our mission is to "provide effective alcohol and other drug dependency services to help women, men and families begin the process of recovery." Since day one when Leonard and I discussed our dream of a new kind of treatment facility, our commitment to this mission has been unfaltering.

I am proud that the Betty Ford Center is viewed by so many as a "beacon of hope" for those seeking treatment for a very complex disease. And I am especially pleased that so many women in particular look to our center as an oasis in the storm.

When my personal journey began at Long Beach Naval Hospital eighteen years ago, most of us women had to participate in male-oriented programs. Because of the strides we have made since that time, my fondest accomplishment is the development of our specialized program designed specifically for women, and today, women represent 50 percent of the Betty Ford Center population.

But no matter who our patients are, or how beautiful our environment is, the very essence of our treatment is the quality of our staff. No one exemplifies this excellence more than my good friend Dr. James West. I can vividly remember Monday, October 4, 1982, when Dr.

West, acting as our admitting physician, welcomed our first four patients. Since that day fourteen years ago, Dr. West has maintained that it is imperative for our physicians to serve as active members of our treatment team. This little bit of insight has prompted Dr. West to develop models of assessment and detoxification that have been duplicated around the world.

In Dr. West, I've found a healer, a teacher, and a friend. He embodies a spirit of commitment and caring. To him, I give my most heartfelt thanks for the encouragement, expertise, and friendship he has given to me personally and to all those who have participated in the Betty Ford Center.

Foreword by John Schwarzlose

On a warm April evening in 1982 in Palm Desert, California, I relaxed in a Jacuzzi with James W. West, M.D., and Joseph Cruse, M.D. These two distinguished physicians and myself had been invited by Mrs. Betty Ford and Leonard Firestone, the cofounders of the Betty Ford Center, to organize and develop the treatment program for the new center.

The three of us had varied backgrounds in the alcohol and drug treatment field. The two physicians had not previously worked in an inpatient treatment center and thus were interested in some of the special nuances of this setting. Under a star-filled sky, we shared our dreams for the Betty Ford Center. But it was clear then as it continues to be clear now that Dr. James West's long and prolific experience in the field of addictive disease was a crucial factor in the successful establishment of the Betty Ford Center.

In the 1970s, Dr. West joined Father Ignatius McDermott in opening Haymarket House, one of the largest and most successful public inebriate programs in the United States. Dr. West also founded and chaired the Illinois State Medical Society's pioneering effort to develop impaired physician programs, as well as assisted religious groups in their intervention with addicted clergy.

I met Dr. West in 1975 in a conference room in a budget motel in Springfield, Illinois, where a group of professionals interested in developing a state-of-the-art system of alcohol and drug counselor credentialing had convened. Prior to these early efforts, most counselors were men or women in recovery who had completed a brief counselor training program. Thus the goal of this credentialing effort was to define the competencies needed to be an effective alcohol and drug counselor. Dr. West's willingness to share his extensive experience and expertise and his participation in this and like efforts were not unusual for him. But for us, his presence was truly special.

Dr. West's pioneering activities were certainly not confined to the addiction field. The BBC recently filmed a story of the first kidney transplant, performed in 1950 at Little Company of Mary Hospital in Chicago, and Dr. West was a prominent member of that transplant team. In the early 1970s, while continuing his surgical practice and training of residents and interns, Dr. West completed specially designed studies in psychiatry; he also participated on boards and committees of various addiction societies in Illinois, including a governor's appointment.

Upon his so-called retirement in 1980 to Rancho Mirage, California, Dr. West again found himself involved in a small treatment facility for alcohol and drug addiction. This serendipitous position developed into something larger when the Betty Ford Center was launched. Dr. West was a prominent member of the Betty Ford Center's planning team and served as its Medical Director from 1983 to 1989. He continues to serve as Physician Director of Outpatient Services. Dr. West has been a member of the Betty Ford Center Board of Directors since 1987 and today is the vice-chairman. He also serves on the Board of Directors of the Eisenhower Memorial Hospital and the Annenberg Center for the Health Sciences.

Dr. West has truly impacted every one of the 28,000 Betty Ford Center alumni. He continues to lecture to the patients once a week on medical aspects of the disease, as well as to the participants in the Family Treatment Program. Time and again, patient satisfaction surveys indicate that Dr. West is the patients' favorite speaker. And in honor of him, donations were received from President and Mrs. Ford and numerous alumni of the Betty Ford Center for the seventh and newest building on our campus, the James W. West Training Center.

Dr. West continues to make incredible contributions to a lifetime of work that goes on and on. Whatever happened to retirement? Dr. West is, by every definition, a man for the ages.

LETTER TO MY READERS

While what you are reading now was never intended to be a book, I'm glad that I've had the opportunity to put the information into this format and get it into the hands of as many readers as possible. The seeds for this project were planted some years ago, when a local newspaper invited the Betty Ford Center to answer questions about alcoholism and drug addiction. Since I was the medical director at the time, John Schwarzlose, the president of the Betty Ford Center, suggested I respond to the mail-in questions, and thus the Q & A column was born. As a practicing surgeon for thirty-five years, I have always seen myself as a caring and clinically effective physician. Since becoming the author of this column, I have experienced a new kind of involvement with the unseen people out there who confided in me and sought my advice, permitting me to share the pain in their lives. I am often moved by their openness and trust, and hope above all that my responses have been helpful and provided some relief.

Unlike my published contributions to the surgical literature, which are rigidly scientific and properly devoid of feeling, my answers to people's questions come from the heart with empathy. My responses are direct, perhaps at times even abrupt, because that's the way surgeons talk to patients who have some grave disorder, lest there be doubt about what should be done. Many of the questions, in fact, most of them, were pages long. I have adapted them, reducing the letters to their bare essentials. Other questions contained details that might expose an abuse victim to harm or violence if published. These I respond to in a way that protects the writer's identity. Other letters were urgent cries for help. These I have tried to answer directly, offering the critical medical advice I believe will help the reader the most.

I hope this book starts you on the path away from a lessening hope and toward a greater day. Take heart!

James W. West, M.D.,
F.A.C.S.

WHO IS AN ALCOHOLIC?

ALCOHOLISM ASSUMES MANY disguises: it takes the form of the homeless drunk, or it looks like the chairman of the board who, only lately, has been making poor corporate decisions; or it may appear as the occasionally hard-to-find physician. It can answer the roll call as a formerly brilliant college senior whose gradually poorer performance predicts the premature end to a promising academic career. It can be the sullen husband whose wife is an expert at covering up an occasional black eye. It languishes in prison for repeated drunk driving arrests. There it was in the Old Testament with Noah and the ark after the flood: "Noah began to be a husbandman, and he planted a vineyard; and he drank of the wine and was drunken" (Genesis 9:20–21). Here it is today in a captain of an oil tanker whose carelessness spoils the shores of Alaska. Then

1

there is the fourth-grade teacher about whom the kids say: "She talks funny sometimes and she goes out of the room a lot, but when she comes back, she's more fun and she laughs a lot. Sometimes she falls down and cries, and the principal has to come in and help her out of the room. He said she was sick. She doesn't teach us anymore."

Alcoholism is a disease of extremes, of disappointments, of depression, of exhilaration, of dishonesty, of denial, of wrecked relationships. Common to all of those who suffer from this disease are a low frustration tolerance, an exquisite sensitivity, a diminished sense of one's own worth, and feelings of isolation that share residence in the head with an elegant set of neurochemical activities the exact reactions of which belong to the alcoholic alone.

Clearly these are the negative extremes that accompany alcoholism. But there is another side of this pendulum: when the alcoholic begins the recovery process, he or she can and will experience a profound joy and sense of gratitude that come with the realization that one has received a new lease on life.

QUESTION: My husband died of alcoholic liver trouble, even though he had not been drinking for several years before he died. Now our son, who is 28, is drinking more, and though I have never seen him intoxicated, I am worried that he may be going the same course that his father did. Can you help?

ANSWER: The following homespun definition of alcoholism may be helpful since it points to the various clues that often indicate the onset of this disease: Alcoholism is defined as the use of alcohol to the extent that it interferes with one's homelife, work, interpersonal relationships, and/or one's health, and its use may be a prerequisite to "feeling normal." Early signs of alcoholism include "relief drinking," preoccupation with drinking, gulping drinks, sneaking drinks, guilty feelings about drinking, refusal to talk about one's drinking, and drinking in spite of strong social, legal, or medical reasons not to drink. Taking a drink to settle one's nerves the "morning after" (or any other time, for that matter), mood swings from happy to sad to angry in rapid cycles, and a driving-under-the-influence charge often indicate the end of the early stage of alcoholism. There follow an increasing tolerance to alcohol and an occasional lapse of memory about what happened while drinking, with lots of promises to loved ones that there's "nothing to worry about." There may be unsuccessful attempts to "cut down" or even quit drinking altogether.

Alcoholism is a progressive illness, moving from early to middle to late stages. It sounds as if your husband was a victim of a late stage of the disease with terminal liver failure, and your son may be experiencing the early gradual onset of the illness. Statistically, the probability that your son will suffer from alcoholism is about 10 to 30 percent, if we simply consider the genetic predisposition to this disease for a son whose father died from alcoholism. Share this information with your son, but be ready for rejection and denial. As mentioned above, these likely reactions are themselves symptoms of alcoholism. It sounds as though you may have spotted very early warning signs here, and the earlier your son is made aware of the dangerous nature of his habit and your concern, the better. Although I have no proof, I have a strong hunch that there are probably many people out there who recognize the dangers their drinking poses and quit successfully before the disease is irreversible without treatment.

QUESTION: I have to admit that after I have a few drinks, I feel normal. I've always felt shy and uncomfortable in social situations, but when I have a few drinks, I begin to feel that I'm okay. I have a responsible job, and over the years have attained a partnership position in a professional firm, but in spite of these accomplishments, I still need to drink in order to feel okay about myself. But, in the past year, I seem to have lost my tolerance to alcohol, and it's harder for me to feel good about myself—the alcohol doesn't seem to "work" anymore. What should I do? I don't want to fall back to once again being that unsociable loner that I used to be. I don't expect an answer, but after a few drinks I thought it would be interesting to hear what you have to say (and also I'm very worried about it).

ANSWER: Alcohol worked for you; now it is betraying you. Remember, it is possible, without alcohol, to have the two absolute requirements for mental health that alcohol seemed to give you at first. These are:

1. A sense of your own worth, and
2. The ability to relate freely and to communicate comfortably with other people.

In other words, you can know who you are and feel okay about yourself, and you can break out of that loneliness to feel socially adequate. Your first drink, then, was a poisonous bit of information: it told you how to get what you yearned for, but in an inevitably destructive way, leading to your alcoholism. Your recovery from this disease through treatment will address all the things about your life related to drinking and the downward direction you describe. First, you must eliminate alcohol before the benefits of psychosocial therapy can begin to take hold. Treatment works. And you will discover that the goal of addiction and the goal of treatment are similar: to feel "normal." But, in recovery, the rewards are permanent and are accompanied by an ever-increasing sense of freedom.

QUESTION: My father died of alcoholism when I was 14 years old. My friends tell me that I can be an alcoholic because this disease is inherited. Is this true?

ANSWER: Yes. There is convincing evidence that alcoholism can be passed along through the generations by way of a biologic pathway called genetic predisposition (Cloninger, C.R. *Journal of Psychiatric Treatment Evaluation* 5 (6): 487–496, 1983). This does not mean that every child of an alcoholic parent will develop alcoholism, but it does mean that the child will be at some risk of developing the disease. It seems that the sons of alcoholics are more frequently afflicted with the disease than the daughters. Although heredity plays an important role in the development of alcoholism, it is fair to say that the majority of children of alcoholics do not become alcoholic. Many authorities in the field believe that environment is as important as heredity in causing alcoholism. But being aware that one's parent was or is an alcoholic may be used in a positive way if the child of the alcoholic is very conscious of the risk involved in deciding to drink alcoholic beverages. After all, it is a perfectly acceptable social decision not to drink alcohol. There is a saying that contains a subtle warning: "If you have to drink to be social, that's not social drinking."

QUESTION: What are the age groups that have the greatest alcohol problems, and does the alcohol abuse rate decline in older people?

ANSWER: I don't know if I can answer those questions with the accuracy that I'd like to, but I can shed some light on them. First, from studies on hospitalized patients reported in *The Journal of the American Medical Association* (September 8, 1993), people in the age group between 45 and 64 years had the highest rate of alcoholism. Those 65 years and older had the next highest occurrence of alcohol problems, and the group with the third highest rate consisted of people from 25 to 44 years of age. Since this data is based upon a select group (i.e., hospitalized patients), it is possible that the actual percentage of alcohol problems may be higher among the youngest group. Common sense would lead us to conclude that these younger people are less likely to be hospitalized for the complications of alcoholism than are those in the older age groups. So we may never have anything near an accurate count of just how many young people are suffering from alcoholism. However, this study did turn up an interesting piece of information on the oldest group. It found that the rate of admission to the hospital for alcoholism among the elderly was at least one third higher than for heart attack.

Question: Are there any reliable predictors of whether a person will become an alcoholic or not?

Answer: Absolute predictors—no. Strong clues—yes. Sons of alcoholics are at much higher risk for developing alcoholism than sons of nonalcoholics. People who demonstrate a low response to alcohol—they can drink more than others without getting drunk—are also at increased risk. These people "who can hold their liquor" seem also to have an increased capacity for drinking from the beginning of their alcohol use. In the case of alcoholic parents who have identical twin children, the chances are very high that if one twin develops alcoholism the other twin will also.

Although these likely candidates for the disease are examples of the genetic, or hereditary, influences, we know that environment plays a significant role, particularly in the late onset of alcoholism. Most professionals in the alcohol treatment field believe that environment acts as a trigger to the onset of alcoholism in an already genetically predisposed person. But so far we have no absolute predictors that will point to those who will definitely develop the disease.

QUESTION: I am 76 years old, and I wake up at least once a night to go to the bathroom. I cannot seem to get back to sleep without drinking about half a bottle of a wine cooler. Am I an alcoholic? I've been thinking of taking a pill to try and help me sleep. What do you think about this?

ANSWER: If that one drink is all you drink, then, no, you are not an alcoholic. But the second question you asked is more serious. I would caution you against taking any sleep medication. Such a substance works only for a few weeks or a month before you have to take more of it to get to sleep, increasing the likelihood that you will develop a dependency on the drug. Furthermore, older folks can be very sensitive to the sedative hypnotic effect of these sleeping pills, and the subsequent dizziness could lead to a fall and possibly a fractured hip. Instead, try an approach that doesn't come in pill form—stay up for a short while, walk around, drink a glass of milk, meditate. One of these methods might work for you and not leave you feeling groggy in the morning as sedatives often can. An insidious kind of chronic alcoholism can start in a 75-year-old with a naturally low tolerance for alcohol and an innocent nightly wine cooler—why take that chance?

QUESTION: Are there many persons in the United States who don't drink any alcoholic beverages?

ANSWER: Yes. It is estimated that about one third of this country's population never drink alcohol. Interestingly, 20 percent of the population consumes 80 percent of all alcohol. More significantly, 7 percent of the population consumes 50 percent of all alcoholic beverages. That 7 percent represents those people who are victims of alcohol dependence or alcohol abuse. However, a bit of good news: there has been a decline in the amount of alcohol consumed in the United States over the past fifteen years.

QUESTION: I drink because of stress. A few drinks used to do the trick. But, in the last couple of years, it takes more to relax me and most of the time I don't get the same relief from my stress that I used to. Sometimes I go beyond that fine line of feeling relaxed and get drunk. My wife has been saying to me and my daughters that I am an alcoholic. I have tried to quit a couple of times, but I can't seem to stop drinking. Also, since my wife started attending Al-Anon meetings, I feel even more stress about the way I choose to relax.

ANSWER: Relief may be at hand, if you trust what I recommend. First, keep in mind that the sedating effect or stress relief alcohol provides for the brain lasts only an hour or so. This temporary relief is followed by long-term—from several hours to a day or so—psychomotor agitation or stress that follows consumption of alcohol. So, based upon this scientific premise, it is clear that you have been taking the wrong medicine for your nerves. When you say you want to quit but can't, you are suggesting that you have lost control over your alcohol use. Quite simply, this is alcoholism. You need treatment, which includes not drinking—believe me, it's possible—and dealing with all of those fears, angers, resentments, agitations, and frustrations related to the stress you are experiencing in your life. The goal of treatment is to remove that powerful need you have to get relief from the bottle and to replace it with a gradually increasing serenity of mind and an alcohol-free body. The road to recovery starts with an admission that you can't drink and that you are powerless over alcohol. A good first step is to call Alcoholics Anonymous in your area.

QUESTION: Let me start by saying that I have been a moderate drinker for years and haven't once before thought I might have a problem. However, on two occasions during the past month, I blacked out and wasn't able to remember anything I said or did after going out with my friends and having about three drinks. The next morning my car was parked in my garage, but I can't even recall driving home. My friends tell me I acted okay and didn't even appear to be drunk. What's happening to my mind? I didn't drink any more than I usually drink on a night out (about five to eight drinks).

11

ANSWER: First off, I would change "moderate drinker" to "alcoholic drinker." One of the most persistent symptoms of alcoholism is the so-called blackout. This usually is experienced by someone who has developed a high physical tolerance to alcohol, which I would identify as a person who can drink five or more drinks with apparently little outward effect. However, during the years this tolerance is developing, the brain is being bathed in alcohol. Further, since alcohol is absorbed into the brain tissue within five minutes, it doesn't take long before the brain is affected. Normally, each conscious experience is received by the brain and encoded so that we can retrieve, or remember, the information when we wish. A brain that has been exposed regularly to enough alcohol, usually about 3 or more ounces, will commonly suffer injury to the central part of the brain where encoding for memory takes place. When the alcohol level is high enough, no memories are recorded. When blood alcohol levels fall, one can again remember what has happened, but for the time when the alcohol level was at a higher level, there is a permanent gap in memory. This is one form of brain damage that gets worse with continued drinking.

I would advise you to stop your drinking. If you have any problem doing so, I would seriously consider getting help.

QUESTION: Are there some nations more prone to alcoholism than others?

ANSWER: It seems that way. People who live in or whose origins are in the northern water countries of Europe appear to drink more and have a higher rate of alcoholism. These countries include Ireland, England, the Scandinavian countries, Germany, France, Poland, and Russia. Countries that border the Mediterranean—Spain, Italy, Greece, Turkey, Israel, Egypt, and North African countries—have lower rates of alcoholism. Asians also tend to have a low incidence of alcoholism as a population. Because many of them lack an enzyme that enables the body to properly metabolize alcohol, they have a very unpleasant reaction to drinking alcohol, including nausea, headaches, quickened pulse, and anxiety.

QUESTION: Is there such a thing as an alcoholic personality?

ANSWER: Yes and no. Specific tests, such as the Edwards Personality Questionnaire (EPQ), that were developed to identify an alcoholic personality have been unreliable, but many professionals who have worked in the field of addictive disease for years have concluded that many alcoholics share traits that could be considered a common personality makeup. They are (1) a low frustration tolerance, (2) sensitivity, (3) a low sense of self-worth, and (4) isolation—a feeling of being different, a "loner." Although these same traits occur in almost every person, in the alcoholic they are exaggerated and have been called the soil for addiction. One could say that alcoholics are like everyone else, but more so. They tend toward the extremes in their feelings, their ambitions, and their drive.

QUESTION: Should everyone be a teetotaler?

ANSWER: No, I don't believe everyone should abstain from drinking entirely, because many people do not have problems controlling their drinking. Some should, however, and they are the people whose use of any amount of alcohol leads immediately or eventually to a total loss of control over the amount of alcohol drunk and who continue to use it in spite of adverse consequences.

QUESTION: I am 46 and have been an alcoholic for many years. I have been told that I have about twelve months left to live with AIDS. My doctor asked me to quit drinking. If I am dying anyway, what difference does it make? I do not care if my time left is shortened or not. The doctor said it was my decision. What would you say?

ANSWER: Even if you really knew how much time you had left, you owe it to yourself to try for the best quality of life possible for you, and that means not drinking alcohol. Alcohol will make worse whatever physical symptoms of AIDS you suffer from and will probably only reinforce the sense of despair that you seem to be feeling. Remember, alcohol is a depressant, and my experience has been that in chronic alcoholic drinking, anxiety and depression are always lurking.

Many people in recovery who are also suffering from AIDS-related symptoms tell me they have experienced an enhanced quality of life in their remaining months and even years, sometimes in spite of severe physical discomfort. They have said that they have found peace and even a kind of joy in their sobriety at this point in their lives. They have mentioned to me that, newly sober, they can feel the support of their family and friends as they never could when they were drinking.

I strongly recommend that you ask your doctor to refer you to an alcohol and drug dependency treatment center, where you can be detoxed. Believe me, there are many recovering alcoholic people with AIDS who have turned alcoholic despair into a heightened quality of life.

What Is the Disease?

A COMMITTEE OF experts in the field of addiction treatment arrived at a consensus for a working definition of alcoholism that is (1) scientifically valid, (2) clinically useful, and (3) understandable by the public. As such, alcoholism can be defined as a chronic disease that carries with it a universally recognizable set of symptoms, including impaired control over drinking, preoccupation with the drug alcohol, use of alcohol despite adverse consequences, and distortions of thinking, most notably denial. These symptoms may be continuous or periodic. And although the disease is often progressive and can be fatal, it is also treatable.

QUESTION: Will you explain the difference between alcohol abuse and alcohol dependence?

ANSWER: In short, alcohol abuse is too much, too often, and alcohol dependence is the inability to quit. Now for some details: *Alcohol abuse* is a pattern of drinking that leads to the failure to fulfill responsibilities at work, home, or school, and/or repeated drinking in situations in which it is physically hazardous—like driving a car, flying an airplane, or similar activities. Abuse is also the case when a person has recurrent alcohol-related legal problems such as arrests for disorderly conduct. If someone continues drinking despite having persistent social and interpersonal problems caused or made worse by the effects of alcohol, including arguments or physical fights with a spouse or friend, that is abuse.

Alcohol dependence may include any or all of the above, but differs from abuse in several fundamental ways. Alcohol dependence is a pattern of alcohol use that can be characterized by a drinker's increase in tolerance—in other words, a need for greater and greater amounts of alcohol to get the desired effect. It can also be signaled by the withdrawal syndrome, which is a cluster of physical and psychological symptoms following the reduction or cessation of drinking or by persistent but unsuccessful attempts to cut down, or even quit drinking altogether. Some individuals suffering from alcohol dependence lose control of their alcohol use and consistently drink more and for longer than intended or can become preoccupied with alcohol and give up important social, occupational, and recreational activities because of it. The cardinal features of alcohol dependence are compulsion (inability to refrain from taking that drink), loss of control over alcohol (can't quit), and continued drinking no matter what the consequences.

QUESTION: Is there more than one kind of alcoholism?

ANSWER: Yes. It appears there are two types of alcoholism, each with its own clinical and hereditary characteristics. The first is called type I alcoholism, and it is characterized by an onset of symptoms usually after the age of 25. It affects males and females equally and seems to be influenced more by environmental factors than heredity. Type I alcoholism is much more common than type II, with a frequency of about 5 to 1, and has a different spectrum of personality traits, including a noticeable psychological dependence on alcohol accompanied by a guilt or fear about this dependence. Type I alcoholics also tend to use alcohol medicinally to relieve anxiety and they generally avoid dangerous or reckless situations.

Type II alcoholism is linked more strongly to heredity, is considerably more severe, and is less influenced by environmental factors. This type of alcoholism occurs mostly in males under the age of 25 and is associated with antisocial traits such as frequent fighting, arrests, and the inability to abstain from drinking. The good news is that both forms are treatable and have similar rates of recovery when treatment is sought (Cloninger, C.R. Neurogenetic Adaptive Mechanisms in Alcoholism. *Science* 236: 410–416, 1987).

QUESTION: You have answered questions about alcoholism, but you haven't said anything about social drinking. What is social drinking?

ANSWER: It is much easier for me to tell you what social drinking is *not* than to tell you what it is. Social drinking is not characterized by a loss of control and progression of continued drinking in spite of adverse consequences. Social drinkers are able to stop drinking permanently if they have some compelling reason for doing so, such as a health issue. Incidentally, even social drinkers can and do develop the medical consequences of alcoholism, such as cirrhosis of the liver and brain damage, if they drink heavily—more than five drinks a day over a long period of time.

It is interesting to note that in 1874, the British physician Francis E. Anstie performed research on the metabolism of alcohol by the body and concluded that "more than two drinks a day could be injurious to one's health." Because of his findings, this physician is remembered as the originator of "Anstie's limit." This may be the first quantitative definition of social drinking. But keep in mind that even two drinks a day may be too much for elderly people who have little tolerance for alcohol and whose metabolism is much slower than that of younger people.

Social drinking may be that drink or two that soften the harsh events of the day or release one to relaxed sociability, or just allow you to see the humor of it all. How many drinks do social drinkers drink? It probably varies. But whatever they do, I can say with certainty that social drinkers don't chase after good feelings by drinking more and more until they lose control. To social drinkers, alcohol is not important, is not necessary to make them feel good, and would not be missed in a nondrinking social setting. They can operate easily with others whether having had drinks or not. Some wise person said, "If you have to drink to be social, that's not social drinking."

QUESTION: What is the SMAST test for alcoholism?

ANSWER: The Short Michigan Alcoholism Screening Test (SMAST) has a greater than 90 percent sensitivity for identifying alcoholism and consists of the following questions:

1. Do you feel you are a normal drinker? (By normal, we mean do you drink less than or as much as most other people?) (No)
2. Do those close to you ever worry or complain about your drinking? (Yes)
3. Do you ever feel guilty about your drinking? (Yes)
4. Do friends or relatives think you are a normal drinker? (No)

5. Are you able to stop drinking when you want to? (No)

6. Have you ever attended a meeting of Alcoholics Anonymous? (Yes)

7. Has drinking ever created problems between you and your wife, husband, a parent, or other near relative? (Yes)

8. Have you ever gotten into trouble at work because of your drinking? (Yes)

9. Have you ever neglected your obligations, your family, or your work for two or more days in a row because you were drinking? (Yes)

10. Have you ever gone to anyone for help about your drinking? (Yes)

11. Have you ever been in a hospital because of drinking? (Yes)

12. Have you ever been arrested for drunken driving, driving while intoxicated, or driving under the influence of alcoholic beverages? (Yes)

13. Have you ever been arrested, even for a few hours, because of other drunken behavior? (Yes)

If your answers match three or more of the parenthetical answers, a diagnosis of alcoholism is indicated; two such answers indicate the possibility of alcoholism; fewer than two answers indicates that alcoholism is not likely. (Reprinted with permission from *Journal of Studies on Alcohol* 36: 124, 1975).

QUESTION: Is the disease concept of alcoholism a new idea?

ANSWER: One hundred or more years before tuberculosis, appendicitis, pneumonia, and diabetes were identified as specific illnesses, alcoholism was described as a disease. In 1785, Dr. Benjamin Rush, a Revolutionary War surgeon, the Father of American Psychiatry, and a signer of the Declaration of Independence, published the classic "Inquiry into the Effects of Ardent Spirits on the Human Body and Mind." In this treatise he explicitly called "the intemperent use of distilled spirits" a disease. He referred to it as "an addiction," and was the first to estimate the rate of death by alcoholism in the United States—"not less than 1,000 people per year in a population of less than 6 million."

QUESTION: What is the oldest recorded instance of alcohol abuse?

ANSWER: As far as I know, it is in the Bible. After the flood waters had receded, "Noah began to be a husbandman, and he planted a vineyard; and he drank of the wine and was drunken" (Genesis 9:20–21).

QUESTION: Why is it some people can drink socially and others drink uncontrollably?

ANSWER: You are really asking what is the cause of alcoholism. That we don't know. There seems to be a sensitivity to alcohol in the brain in those who are susceptible to the disease. In those prone to alcoholism, alcohol provides a powerful positive response that effectively meets a psychological need. Repeatedly satisfying this powerful mental or emotional yearning provides the reinforcement that is an essential part of all addictions.

Neurochemical reactions in the brain of people who drink uncontrollably are very probably unique to the alcoholic. Recent research has revealed how brain neurotransmitters, receptors, and calcium and chloride ion channels react to alcohol. The difference in how these neurophysiological phenomena respond to alcohol in the nonalcoholic drinker and the alcoholic drinker is probably driven by the genetic makeup of the individuals in question.

But this brain chemistry is just part of the picture. In addition to all of this is the triad of behavioral characteristics that the alcoholic is predisposed to as well: compulsion, loss of control, and that peculiar mental state that exists even before the first drink, which is demonstrated by the continued use of alcohol in spite of adverse consequences. We don't have the whole answer: essentially, there is no "cure" for alcoholism, just an arrest of the disease. But we do have remarkably successful treatment—I guess we should be thankful for that.

QUESTION: Just exactly what is alcohol withdrawal? I am not an alcoholic but a few hours after I drink a few beers, I get irritable, testy, and just feel punk. Is there any way to prevent this?

ANSWER: There is, but you won't like it. Alcohol in your beer is a depressant and mitigates your normal levels of arousal and alertness. At first, a few drinks may feel stimulating, but the basic site of the depressant action is in the reticular activating system in the stem of the brain. As you drink more beers, there is a greater depressant effect, and as you require more alcohol to arrive at the desired feeling, you develop a tolerance. Then, when you stop drinking and your blood alcohol level goes down, you experience a rebound hyperactivity-alertness. This is commonly known as the hangover. How mild or serious it is and how long your hangover lasts are directly proportional to how much and how long you have been drinking.

There are four stages of the acute alcohol withdrawal syndrome. Stage I is characterized by a slight tremor, jumpy, edgy, irritable, and sweaty feelings, a fast pulse, and the inability to sleep. Stage II includes all of the above plus some hallucinations—seeing and hearing things that aren't there. Stage III consists of a very rapid heartbeat, a high temperature, delusions, disorientation or psychotic behavior, and severe tremulousness. In spite of available medical care, 10 to 20 percent of those people with stage III (delirium tremens) usually die during the episode. Stage IV is characterized by convulsions also known as rum fits. A seizure precedes the D.T.'s in one third of those who experience this stage of withdrawal. So, as you can see, the withdrawal syndrome progresses from one stage to another as drinking becomes greater in quantity and more prolonged. The only way to prevent it is to stop drinking.

QUESTION: Can loneliness be a cause of alcoholism?

ANSWER: Some people drink to relieve the pain of their loneliness. However, loneliness by itself is not the cause of alcoholism and does not necessarily lead to compulsive drinking, but it can be a catalyst. If a person suffering from loneliness develops alcoholism, it usually means that that person has a genetic predisposition to the disease. The fact that widowers comprise the group with the highest percentage of alcoholism means loneliness must play a role in this disease and that your question is a good one. But looking at all we know about alcoholism, I would say that loneliness is a factor but not a cause of alcoholism.

QUESTION: I lived on the street for a time after I lost my job. Out there, if they can't get anything else, some people drink rubbing alcohol. I've drunk some of the stuff myself, but I stopped after I saw my friend die after drinking a pint. What's in rubbing alcohol that is so bad?

ANSWER: Rubbing alcohol is not ethyl alcohol (beverage alcohol), but isopropyl alcohol, a totally different chemical than the alcohol of beer, wine, or liquor. When the liver breaks down this kind of alcohol, it turns into acetone, a poison. If rubbing alcohol is ingested, the result is a deep coma, and often kidney failure. The lethal dose of isopropyl alcohol by mouth in adult humans is about 8 ounces. Another kind of poison is wood alcohol, found in windshield washer fluids, shellac thinner, and canned fuel used to heat foods on a buffet table. This is methyl alcohol, and it breaks down in the liver to formaldehyde; those who survive after drinking it often suffer permanent blindness. As little as 2 ounces of wood alcohol can be fatal.

QUESTION: What is meant by *proof* when referring to alcoholic beverages?

ANSWER: The word *proof* came about years ago when ships, unloading their cargo of whiskey, had only one way to tell the strength of the liquor they were carrying. They mixed a spoonful of whiskey with a pinch of gunpowder. When a lighted match was dropped into the mixture, it ignited with an audible "proof"! This microfireworks would happen only if the alcohol content was 50 percent or more by volume. Today *proof* is defined as twice the alcohol content by volume. Whiskey with 50 percent alcohol is 100-proof whiskey. There are better ways of determining alcohol content by volume these days, but they aren't as much fun as the old-fashioned way.

QUESTION: Are death rates from alcohol consumption that high? They seem to be exaggerated. Would you address this please?

ANSWER: They aren't exaggerated. Alcohol-related conditions, particularly those that are contributing rather than direct causes of death, are substantially underreported on death certificates. This may be due to a reporting bias, lack of information on the deceased person's drinking history, or both. Chronic alcohol-related liver disease, which provides organic evidence at an autopsy, ranks as the ninth leading cause of death in the United States.

Alcohol-related deaths commonly come disguised as

trauma. The leading cause of injury deaths in the United States in 1987 (46,386) was motor vehicle crashes. Half of these were alcohol related. Unintentional falls are the second leading cause of fatal injury in the United States, accounting for about 13,000 deaths a year. One study reports that about 40 percent of fatalities due to falls are alcohol related (Andra, R., et al. Alcohol and Fatal Injuries Among U.S. Adults. *Journal of the American Medical Association* 260: 2529–2532, 1988). The third leading cause of accidental death in the United States is drowning, and research findings suggest the victims had been drinking alcohol in about 38 percent of drowning deaths. Fires and burns are the fourth leading cause of accidental deaths in the United States and account for 6,000 fatalities a year. A large number of studies report a great increase in alcohol-related deaths from burns, with some concluding that 48 percent of fire and burn victims were intoxicated at the time of the fatal accident.

Further, research indicates that 20 to 36 percent of suicide victims have a history of alcohol abuse and were drinking shortly before their suicide. Also, these studies show that alcohol-related suicides often seem to be impulsive rather than premeditated, and that there is a relation among alcohol, suicide, and firearms, which tends to make an attempt more surely fatal.

All of the evidence I have come across leads me to believe that alcohol is every bit the danger that it has been made out to be—if not more so.

QUESTION: On what scientific evidence do you base your statement that alcoholism is a disease? As a practicing physician, I have always thought persons who drank to excess did so because they wanted to, and yet, I'm trying to keep an open mind that there may be more to it than that.

ANSWER: Believe me, Doctor, there is. Let's start with the basic definition of disease that assumes all diseases have a harmful effect on the body or mind, or both, and each disease has a train of signs and symptoms that we as clinicians can use to differentiate one disease from another. Alcoholism possesses a unique profile: gradually progressive loss of control over alcohol use, a preoccupation with acquiring alcohol, a continued use in spite of adverse consequences, and a pattern of relapse to alcohol consumption. These are irrefutable symptoms, whether in a steady or periodic pattern, and are universal to all victims of the illness.

As with other diseases, there are different intensities of alcoholism but the root characteristics are common to all: compulsion, loss of control, and continued use in spite of adverse consequences. All of these symptoms are behavioral, but some may have a physiological basis such as an initial increased tolerance to alcohol or an especially positive response to alcohol that may be a function of the neurotransmitter system in the brain.

Further indications that alcoholism is a disease are the conclusion of familial and genetic studies that traced twins separated at birth. It was observed that alcoholism is an inherited primary disorder and operates independently of other personality and psychiatric disorders. Evidence continues to surface pointing to the fact that the relationship between brain chemistry and behavior is more than likely genetic.

INTERVENTION AND DEALING WITH LOVED ONES

Any intervention interrupts the progression of a disease. It can be surgery for the treatment of appendicitis, or antibiotics in the care of pneumonia. With any disease, intervention interrupts our inevitable path toward death. It is important to keep in mind that alcoholism and drug addiction are both diseases that can kill. So when you are worried about a loved one whose problem has gotten out of control, seek help for them and for you! You are completely warranted in your concern. Alcoholism and drug abuse can turn very quickly into a life-or-death situation.

For those alcoholics or drug abusers who are reluctant or refuse treatment, a formal intervention is a recommended way of forcing the troubled person to seek help. A formal intervention begins first with obtaining the services of a professional interventionist (contact any treatment center or psychiatrist for a referral). The professional interventionist then gathers the alcoholic's (or drug addict's) concerned family, employers, and/or close friends at a meeting where together the group rehearses how to confront the alcoholic. The loved ones write brief (one or two sentences) statements, describing how the alcoholic's drinking has affected them. It is crucial that, prior to the actual intervention, arrangements are made for the alcoholic to enter a treatment facility directly following the intervention. At the intervention, the loved ones then read aloud their respective statements to the alcoholic in the presence and under the guidance of the professional interventionist. Such formal interventions have an 80 percent success rate.

QUESTION: Is there any special technique in getting a person who seems to be getting by with his heavy drinking to quit? My husband refuses to talk about his drinking and it is wrecking our family life.

ANSWER: Most of the time it is difficult to convince people who seem to be "getting by" that they are alcoholics. First of all, they are protecting themselves from accepting that they have a problem by using denial, one of our most powerful defense mechanisms. I would suggest trying to discuss with your husband the signs of early alcoholism that he may be demonstrating, including an increase in alcohol tolerance, temporary memory loss while drinking, sneaking drinks and hiding liquor, drinking fast or gulping drinks, anger or refusal to talk about his drinking, and perhaps an increasing frequency of intoxication. These are signs of alcoholism, which is not only an inevitably progressive disease but an exquisitely predictable one. If you discuss these signs with your husband as you see them appear in his drinking behavior, you may move him to seek help. Unfortunately, I think it is much more likely that it will be necessary for you to get professional assistance in setting up a formal intervention. You can do this by calling an alcoholism treatment center for a referral to an interventionist who will evaluate your need and arrange the scenario for the intervention and the referral to treatment.

Whether these efforts are successful or not, I strongly recommend that you, the questioner, enter a family treatment program to deal with your own emotional health and possible codependence. You are most likely going through all kinds of stress you might not even be aware of as a result of your husband's drinking. The healthier and stronger you are, the more support you will be able to provide for him if he chooses to get help.

Question: My wife is in treatment for alcoholism. I tried to defend some of her bizarre behaviors while she was drinking, and now a friend of mine, who himself is a recovering alcoholic, says that I am a codependent. What is that? He suggest treatment for me in the family program at the place where she is getting treatment. I rarely drink at all, but I'll do anything to help her.

Answer: Family treatment probably would be very helpful for you. Many spouses of alcoholics are codependent, that is, they may unwittingly contribute to their spouses' difficulty in recovery from alcoholism. For instance, you may, like many people in your position, change who you are to please others, feel responsible for meeting other people's needs at the expense of your own, suffer from low self-esteem, be driven by compulsion, and also be in denial as to the extent or nature of the alcoholism in your household. After a day or two of family therapy, often the person close to the alcoholic begins to identify with these traits; this could lead to you getting the emotional support and understanding you need to deal with the backlash of your spouse's illness.

It is my experience that when one person in a household is an alcoholic, everyone is affected, and everyone's reaction to the alcoholic's behavior can reinforce the overall problem. By seeking support in a family treatment program, you will learn how to separate yourself from your spouse's behavior and consequently feel better equipped to help her recover and get well.

QUESTION: My husband absolutely refuses to hear anything about his drinking. He has also refused to get any kind of help. I've been told there is something that I can put in his coffee that will make him sick if he drinks. Do you know of any such thing? Will it work? My daughters and I are desperate.

ANSWER: Don't try it. First of all, it could be dangerous and second, there is yet to be any proof of success with this substance. The drug you are referring to is disulfiram (or Antabuse), which when taken within twelve to eighteen hours before drinking alcohol produces a physical response within five minutes consisting of throbbing in the head, flushing, severe rapid heartbeat, shortness of breath, nausea, vomiting, and loss of balance. It could be that your husband may agree to see a physician, and after a physical examination accept the idea of taking care of this problem by himself with the help of disulfiram, which he would take in a prescribed safe dose and voluntarily. However, you may want to consider some other options, including calling a treatment center to find out about an intervention for him, which works about 80 percent of the time.

Be sure that you and your daughters become involved in a family/Al-Anon program no matter what else happens. These kinds of programs help deal with the emotional fallout from one person's alcoholism. Often, members of an alcoholic's family experience a range of negative feelings directed at the alcoholic and themselves, including pain, anger, frustration, and shame.

Question: My mother and father both drink, and I consider their drinking heavy. They drink almost every night to the point where they act silly and even slur their words. I have tried to talk about this to them, but they refuse. I won't have other kids over because, in a way, I feel ashamed of my parents. Lately, they have been very angry when I bring up things I've been taught about alcohol in my eighth-grade classes.

Answer: You are a good and courageous daughter or son. You are not alone, and there is help with this difficult situation you are facing with your family. First of all, although your parents probably have alcoholism, you are not the cause of their drinking. Try to remember that your parents are suffering from an illness and that you did not make them sick. I bring this up even though you did not because many kids of alcoholic parents spend countless hours with this "secret worry." However, I understand that your parents' drinking is making you unhappy. There are solutions to this, but they don't start out with your parents being "cured." I think you may feel better able to cope with the situation if you speak with someone like a school counselor, a teacher, or a minister or priest at your church. Remember, too, that your parents' problem has now become your problem and that you will not be betraying your loyalty to them by going to someone and asking for their support and understanding. Or, perhaps it would be easier to start out by calling an organization of people such as Alateen (800) 344-2666, or the National Association of Children of Alcoholics (301) 468-0985.

You can just call that number and talk. Conversations you have during these calls are held in the strictest confidence.

QUESTION: Our daughter is an alcoholic. We have suffered with her ailment for some thirty years. In desperation, should we persuade her to take Prozac?

ANSWER: I don't know. I can sense the pain in your letter and I wish I could tell you that Prozac might help, but this drug is effective for an altogether different disease. Prozac is an antidepressant that increases the amount of the neurotransmitter serotonin, which can help lift the feelings of depression in people who can't seem to break out of a continual black mood themselves. Prozac has also been prescribed for anxiety. However, though depression and anxiety may accompany alcoholism, they are not intrinsic to the disease. Your daughter requires a physical and mental evaluation to determine the exact nature of her condition. If the primary disorder is identified as alcoholism, then Prozac may not be appropriate. If she suffers from a dual disorder—depression, major anxieties, phobias, manic-depressive disorder, or psychosis, in addition to alcoholism—she may require a specific psychoactive nonaddicting medication.

Has she ever been in alcoholism treatment? Tried A.A.? There are a number of options in spite of a thirty-year history of alcoholism, and all have the goal of recovery. Finally, have you and your spouse been through a family program to try to let go of some of the acute pain that I know you must be feeling? You may have heard all of this before, but don't give up— many times treatment for an alcoholic and her family can work the second or third time around.

THE BRAIN

THIS THREE-POUND organ is where the drama of alcoholism and drug addiction takes place. Like a symphony orchestra, the neurological circuits, the neurotransmitters, and the receptors are all highly tuned and respond to each incoming chemical in a different but oh so glorious way. But, this is also the place of gloom where the music dies down when addictive drugs and alcohol have run their course.

Activity in the normal brain moves along at a regular, rather predictable pace, determining who we are, what we do, and how we do it. There are regulators that control bodily functions and the senses—hearing, sight, taste, smell, and touch. Dependent on all of these physical characteristics, but above them, is cognition, which can best be defined as learning, remembering, and being able to recall and use this knowledge. Bright people are particularly gifted in their realm of thinking whereas lesser minds are more limited in their range of mental functioning. But, smart or dull, alcohol and other drugs can injure this uniquely human faculty.

Brain function studies of chronic alcoholics who had stopped drinking for weeks or so before testing often demonstrate long-lasting deficits in four areas of functioning in the brain: abstract thought and problem-solving skills, verbal skills and/or memory, dexterity of movement, and visiospatial skills. Researchers most often connect these impairments of function with the right hemisphere of the brain (Parsons, O.A. Impaired Neuropsychological Cognitive Functioning in Sober Alcoholics, in Hunt, W.A., and Nixon, S.J., eds. *Alcohol Induced Brain Damage*. National Institute on Alcohol Abuse and Alcoholism. Research Monograph No. 22, NIH Publication No. 93-3549: 173–194, 1993). Magnetic resonance imaging (MRI) of the brain reveals a consistent shrinkage of brain tissue depending on the amount and duration of heavy alcohol consumption (Jernigan, T.L., et al. Reduced Gray Matter Observed in Alcoholics Using Magnetic Resonance Imaging. *Alcoholism: Clinical and Experimental Research* 15 (3): 418–427, 1991). But it is encouraging to know that there is some degree of recovery of thinking and behavioral functioning with permanent discontinued drinking. Indeed, one study showed that repeated mental exercises seem to speed improvement (Goldman, M.S. Recovery of Cognitive Functioning in Alcoholics. *Alcohol Health and Research World* 19 (2): 148–154, 1995). The brain, like the rest of the body, is resilient and has a natural drive to restore its health.

QUESTION: What happens in the brain when you drink alcohol?

ANSWER: At that point, lots of things are happening in the brain. Everyone who has observed a person who is drunk has witnessed the effect of alcohol on behavior and physical functioning. For centuries, we have known that alcohol acts as a depressant and we once even used it as an anesthetic, demonstrating its power to sedate feeling in the body. But in general, drinks number one, two, and three affect the cerebral cortex of the brain, which is the location of our higher mental function. This first level of alcohol consumption also affects the reticular activating system, which controls our alertness and automatic responses to our environment and on which we rely heavily for safe driving. Drinks three or four or five affect the back of the brain—the cerebellum—and interfere with our motor (muscle) movements. At first we lose the capacity for fine motion, and then later we experience a gross loss of coordination. Drinks five to seven work deep in the brain at a place called the midbrain and limbic system, where functions such as appetite, sexual activity, and a major component of memory are located. In this limbic area there also resides the primitive emotional makeup of humans: anger, fright, territoriality, the functions of hierarchy, or "pecking order," and sexual function. Here is the area that often makes the maudlin drunk so all-loving and teary. Finally, drinks seven, eight, nine, or more strike at the deepest part of the brain, the medulla, the site of the respiratory control center. In acute alcohol overdose, the respiratory center shuts down, and the victim stops breathing.

These amounts of alcohol, if drunk within an hour or two by the average person, are sufficient to bring about this irregularly descending depressant effect on the central nervous system. In other, more alcohol-tolerant persons, an additional drink or so at each stage will inevitably produce these dire effects. But alcohol poisoning and death can occur from rapid drinking of from 1 pint to 1 fifth of 100-proof liquor or "chug-a-lugging" ten to sixteen cans of beer. A large amount of alcohol rapidly ingested can equal death.

QUESTION: Recently, a friend of mine, a recovering alcoholic who has not had a drink for more than thirty years, underwent a serious heart operation. The operation was successful but after three days, he began to see and hear things that weren't there, similar to the D.T.'s he suffered years ago after prolonged drinking bouts. Is his reaction to the surgery connected with those old drinking days? I repeat, this man has not had a drink for over thirty years.

ANSWER: There is a connection. Occasionally, a person who has experienced severe stage III acute withdrawal syndrome from alcohol, what you are calling the D.T.'s, or delirium tremens, in the past is susceptible to a re-

turn of some of the symptoms of this condition following a major operation or severe injury with massive
tissue damage. The exact neurophysiological mechanism of this phenomenon is not known. It has been
speculated that during the initial bouts of D.T.'s, some
brain change occurs, creating a kind of memory that is
reactivated following a major biological shock to the
body, such as a major operation or severe injury. It is
also conceivable that medications used during anesthesia for an operation could use some of the same neurological circuitry that had been trodden upon so heavily
during your friend's former drinking days. This kind of
postoperative or posttraumatic occurrence is characterized by either auditory or visual hallucinations, or a
combination of both, without the very dangerous wild
racing of the vital signs of actual D.T.'s—rapid pulse,
high temperature, high blood pressure, and marked
tremulousness. The condition is usually easily managed
with minimal amounts of sedation for the short period
of time the hallucinations last. It is of prime importance
in the care of the surgical patient that the surgeon take
a careful history of alcohol use and its past consequences (D.T.'s). In this way, the physician can antici-
pate the reemergence of that possibly severe condition
and prevent it with postoperative medication.

QUESTION: What is meant by a "wet brain"?

ANSWER: Good question. The term *wet brain* is not scientifically valid, but refers to a very real condition known as Wernicke-Korsakoff syndrome. This chronic brain syndrome is caused by long-term alcoholism and is accompanied by a triad of symptoms: (1) mental disturbance; (2) confusion, drowsiness, and paralysis of eye movements; and (3) ataxia, or a staggering gait. A primary cause for this is a thiamine (vitamin B_1) deficiency due to severe malnutrition and poor intestinal absorption of food and vitamins caused by alcohol. The wet-brain person acts much like the Alzheimer's victim with loss of recent memory, disorientation with regard to time and place, confusion, and confabulation, or telling imagined and untrue experiences as truth. If wet brain is identified in its early onset, an infusion of thiamine (B_1) may have some preventive value. But, unfortunately, there is no recovery from Wernicke-Korsakoff syndrome; therefore, it is one of the most tragic consequences of alcoholism.

QUESTION: I think of myself as a moderate drinker—two or three drinks a day, more on the weekends—but it has never interfered with my work, nor does my family think I have a problem. Three weeks ago I was at a gathering of friends and had a few more drinks than usual, and the following day I was not able to remember anything about the previous evening. My wife tells me that I appeared to be normal and did not act drunk in any way. This concerns me very much. I am 57 years old. Can only five or so drinks cause this?

ANSWER: Well, it seems they did. What you experienced, but can't recall, is an alcohol blackout, which involves two levels of memory. Short-term, or immediate, memory is stored electrically, and lasts for about twenty minutes. During this crucial time, the electrical form of memory is converted in the brain to long-term chemical memory by a phenomenon called encoding. Alcohol has the capacity to interfere with this remarkable process, so that short-term electrical configuration of what one perceives never becomes permanent and consequently can't be retrieved from memory because it isn't there. This amnesia occurs in people whose drinking has been somewhat more than moderate for a long time. Several other things can produce this frightening state of affairs: brain concussion, severe electrical shock, and anesthesia.

QUESTION: Around about twelve hours after my last drink of my last two binges, I began to see things and hear threatening voices that I knew weren't there. The visions left after about twelve hours, but the voices still come back every now and then. Was this the D.T.'s? Is this going to happen every time I drink?

ANSWER: No, this was not the D.T.'s (delirium tremens), and yes, it probably will happen every time after you come off a binge. This reaction, alcoholic hallucinosis, occurs in people with a long drinking history, but why the brain responds in this particular way to this stage of alcohol withdrawal is not completely understood. Having visions or hallucinations is uncommon and happens to some otherwise healthy people who are long-term heavy drinkers. Fortunately, this condition is not accompanied by the severe physical and mental complications of delirium tremens, but it can be very frightening to have auditory or visual hallucinations even six months after the last drink.

QUESTION: What is the connection between posttraumatic stress disorder (PTSD) and alcoholism?

ANSWER: An ex–Marine officer who provides therapy for Vietnam veterans with posttraumatic stress disorder (PTSD) reports that many of those he has treated also have an alcohol abuse problem. PTSD refers to the cluster of pathological symptoms characterized by the painful mental and emotional response initiated by the recall of a deeply imprinted traumatic memory. These painful memories can intrude on a person's consciousness with or without cues, and in some persons they seem to grow more vivid and stronger with time. Research has shown that when these memories are deliberately evoked, the subjects experience physiological changes, including a rapid heartbeat, sweating, overall weakness, shakiness, and a feeling of hyperalertness. There doesn't appear to be a direct connection between PTSD and alcoholism except that a person who is a victim of this often disabling disorder may drink excessively to dull the pain and anguish of these persistent and obtrusive disturbing memories. However, drinking not only does not help, but it interferes with the specific psychotherapy necessary for dealing with PTSD—the two conditions require separate treatment.

Question: If alcoholism has a high death rate, why is it classified as a mental illness? I thought people died of physical diseases.

Answer: They do, so alcohol combines the elements of both mental illness and physical disease. Alcoholism is classified as a substance abuse disorder in the *Diagnostic and Statistical Manual of Mental Disorders* (*DSM-III*). Mental and emotional symptoms of alcoholism exist long before the grave physical complications of the disease appear. The mental symptoms consist of loss of control (taking in larger amounts of alcohol over a longer period of time than the person intends); persistent desire to drink (one or more unsuccessful efforts to cut down or control drinking); continued drinking in spite of adverse social, occupational, or legal consequences; and frequent intoxication or withdrawal symptoms when expected to fulfill major obligations at work, school, or home. These are all behavioral or mental symptoms, which, unless interrupted permanently by treatment, will inevitably lead to physical complications of alcoholism. Cirrhosis of the liver, chronic brain deterioration, and other grave organic consequences occur as a result of long-term heavy drinking, but the core of the disease is the cluster of behavioral symptoms that constitute the mental disorder called alcoholism. Consequently, the treatment of alcoholism targets the mind rather than any physical system. So alcoholism and all other substance abuse disorders are mental disorders, with a high physical complication rate.

QUESTION: Does drinking alcohol really cause brain damage? So many people drink and enjoy it, and the people I know don't seem to have anything the matter with them.

ANSWER: It's possible that you don't know any long-term heavy drinkers. Alcohol—whiskey, wine, beer, or any other kind of alcoholic drink—causes brain damage depending upon how much is drunk and for how long. Over time alcohol causes brain atrophy or shrinkage, which correlates in psychological tests to significant impairments in problem solving, perception, and memory. In other words, alcoholic brain damage means lower general intelligence, poorer verbal learning and poorer understanding of the spoken or written word, and overall impoverishment of language. Brain damage is more pronounced in middle-aged or older alcoholics. For women, a brain scan abnormality similar to that found in males appears after significantly shorter and less intense drinking histories. This pattern is consistent with findings for other alcohol-induced organ damage in women, such as liver disease. So, yes, alcoholic beverages cause brain damage depending on how much is drunk and for how long. Certainly, four or more drinks on a regular daily basis over an extended period of time puts the brain tissue at risk of harm.

THE BODY

ALCOHOL AND OTHER drugs are handled by the body in the same way that foods or other substances are processed. Some addicting drugs have a harmful effect after long-term use; others don't harm the organs. These chemicals are metabolized in the liver and are eventually excreted. However, before they are passed out of the body, they move by way of the bloodstream to the target organ of their activity, the brain. Aside from the brain and the liver, the major organs and systems affected by alcohol abuse are the pancreas, esophagus, stomach, peripheral nerves, and blood. All addicting drugs activate the "reward and craving" neurological pathways of the brain, and therein lies their addictability.

Long-term alcohol and tobacco use account for approximately 115,000 and 425,000 deaths, respectively, in this country each year. However, the body is resilient. If one survives the warfare of active addiction, abstinence from these drugs can lead to acceptable or even perfect health. But, recovery from addiction must include principles of good nutrition, exercise, and treatment of residual damage to the body from smoking or drinking.

QUESTION: What nutritional value does alcohol have?

ANSWER: None. Alcohol provides 7 empty calories per gram without any nutritional value and actually can interfere with our body's ability to get some nutrients from other food we eat. There seems to be decreased intestinal absorption of vitamin B and folic acid with chronic alcoholism, along with reduced plasma transport of vitamins due to diminished plasma proteins resulting from liver disease and malnutrition. Decreased tissue uptake and storage of vitamin B_1 may play a role in alcoholic brain damage associated with the Wernicke-Korsakoff syndrome. In fact, one very significant cause of nervous-system destruction in chronic alcoholism is the vulnerability of the sensitive nervous system to malnutrition.

Question: What is an alcoholic liver? My uncle died and my cousin told me he had an alcoholic liver. Can you explain?

Answer: The liver is the organ most involved in the metabolism of alcohol. If eight 12-ounce cans of beer, or the equivalent in wine or 80-proof liquor, is consumed daily over a period of eight to twelve months, an inflammation of the liver called alcoholic hepatitis will occur. The condition is often reversible if the person stops drinking. However, with continued drinking, alcoholic hepatitis progresses to cirrhosis of the liver, in which the liver tissue becomes replaced by scar tissue. Cirrhosis of the liver is one of the most common causes of death in the United States. About 67 percent of people with it will survive if they stop drinking. Those afflicted who continue to drink usually die from liver disease or one of its complications. The only effective treatment for this condition is abstinence from alcohol. Some people are more susceptible to cirrhosis than others. Women are more at risk to develop liver disease than men, even though they may drink lesser amounts per pound of body weight. Physicians diagnose alcoholic liver disease by physical examination, laboratory blood tests, and needle liver biopsy.

QUESTION: I have been taking high blood pressure medicine for years and my blood pressure continued to be high. I stopped drinking nine months ago and my physician says that my blood pressure has gone down to normal. Does alcohol cause high blood pressure?

ANSWER: There certainly is a connection. A review of thirty studies reported significant elevation in blood pressure in individuals who consumed an average of three standard drinks a day (MacMahon, S. Alcohol Consumption and Hypertension. *Hypertension* 9 (2): 111–121, 1987). A standard drink would be a 12-ounce can of beer, a regular mixed drink, or a 5-ounce glass of wine. Among the risk factors for high blood pressure in men, alcohol is second only to obesity. Several studies have shown that men with high blood pressure experience a reduction in blood pressure when they lower alcohol consumption. Medical consequences of high blood pressure include stroke, heart disease, and other related disorders, all of which may be fatal. If alcohol contributes to the cause of high blood pressure, which in turn leads to death by any of the above, one can conclude that there is indeed a mortal connection between high blood pressure and alcohol.

Question: I am 46 years old and have been competitive in local and even some national women's amateur athletic tournaments. I am also a recovering alcoholic with seven years of sobriety behind me. I have noticed in the past year that my endurance has decreased and I seem to get short of breath more quickly than my contemporaries with whom I've been competing all these years. I have checked with my doctor a number of times and she says that there doesn't seem to be anything wrong. I have not told the doctor about my previous heavy drinking because I have been sober so long. Do you have any suggestions?

Answer: Tell her! Alcohol has a distinct effect on the heart and other muscles when heavy drinking has extended over a long period of time. Not only does the heart become enlarged and the heart muscle weaker, but all the arm and leg muscles become weaker over time as well. Studies show that alcohol damages muscle tissue in both men and women, but more frequently in women, with only 60 percent of the lifetime alcohol intake and in less time than in men. Give your doctor a chance to help with these symptoms by telling her about your drinking past so that she can order the appropriate tests for you. There may be some things, in addition to your continued sobriety, she will recommend to help you get back your competitive edge.

QUESTION: My father recently died in the hospital following an auto accident in which he suffered multiple injuries and sepsis, or overall infection throughout the body and the blood. The physicians who attended him claim that one of the most significant conditions he developed was a lung condition that eventually was the cause of his death. The reason I am writing is that the doctor said that this lung condition was probably brought on by my father's longtime chronic heavy alcohol consumption. Can you comment on this?

ANSWER: Your father may have developed a lung condition called acute respiratory distress syndrome, which occurs as a complication in many persons who have grave illnesses. It occurs more frequently in chronic alcoholics with the at-risk diseases or traumas than in persons who do not have a history of heavy, long-term drinking. Not only does the condition happen more frequently in alcoholics, but when it does occur, the death rate is twice as high as in those who have not been chronic alcohol consumers. (*Journal of the American Medical Association*, Jan. 3, 1996, Marc Moss et al.)

QUESTION: My mother, who is 48 years old and drinks five or six glasses of wine a day, developed severe pain in her right hip. X rays showed that she had what the doctor called deterioration of the hip bone. He says it's from alcohol. Could you comment on this?

ANSWER: Your mother has a condition that occurs in 5 to 10 percent of alcoholics. It is characterized by a deterioration of bone near the hip joint due to a sudden loss of blood supply. This loss is often caused by a clot in the blood vessel that supplies blood to the bone (the femoral head) or an inflammation of the blood vessels called vasculitis. This condition results from heavy alcohol use and is called avascular necrosis. It commonly requires a hip joint replacement depending on the severity of the bone death. If your mother's drinking continues, studies show that her shoulder and knee could be affected in a similar manner within three years.

QUESTION: I've heard it said that if drunk long enough and in large enough amounts, alcohol has a feminizing effect on the male. Is this true or not?

ANSWER: True. But what you may not know is that it does this by way of liver damage. After a number of years of drinking heavily and often after suffering repeated bouts of alcoholic hepatitis and the inevitable cirrhosis of the liver, men also experience alcohol-related damage to the testicular tissue. This causes a decrease in the amount of their circulating testosterone. So, the combination of these two tissue injuries leads to the condition of hyperestrogenism, increased circulating female hormone from natural stores in the damaged liver, and hypoandrogenism, decreased circulating male hormone. The feminizing effect of this condition can result in loss of hair on the chest and upper body, loss of facial hair, and enlarged, femalelike breasts.

QUESTION: I am a 57-year-old retired executive. I have been a social drinker all my life, but since retiring I have upped my drinking to about 8 or so ounces of vodka spread over the day. About three months ago, I noticed a kind of numbness in my feet. Is this from alcohol? The doctor says it is.

ANSWER: I believe your doctor is right. Alcohol has a direct toxic effect on the nerve fibers in the legs and arms. Alcohol can cause the degeneration of the myelin insulation of the nerve fiber as the nerve "dies back" from the feet and hands toward the upper leg and arm, accompanied by a loss of sensation in the hands and feet. Also, painful feet and weakness of the thigh muscle are part of the progression of this alcoholic polyneuropathy. Excessive sweating in the face and neck may also occur as a result of this condition. About 10 percent of hospitalized alcoholics experience this condition, which usually improves with abstinence, but slowly. Alcohol is the cause—no alcohol is the treatment.

QUESTION: My husband was a heavy drinker until three months ago when he became very sick. He was put on a dialysis machine because his kidneys failed. The doctor said this was due to the effect of alcohol on his muscles. Can you explain?

ANSWER: Hold on! The condition was probably acute alcoholic rhabdomyolysis, which is caused by the effect of alcohol on muscle tissue. When the muscle dies in this way, it releases a by-product called myoglobin, which has a toxic effect on the kidneys, causing kidney failure. This rather rare condition is sometimes reversible without treatment, but it always recurs with resumed drinking.

QUESTION: I have been operated on for breast cancer. The doctors believe they were able to get all of the cancer, but they have recommended cancer chemotherapy as an added precaution. In light of my bout with cancer, is there any reason I cannot have a drink on occasion? I do not have an alcohol problem.

ANSWER: Yes, there is a very convincing reason you should not drink alcohol. Recent reports show that there is a much greater progression of cancer in animals exposed to alcohol (equivalent to four or five drinks a day) than in those animals with cancer not exposed to alcohol (Alcohol and Cancer: Alcohol Alert. National

Institute of Alcohol and Alcohol Abuse, No. 21 PH 345, July 1993). Alcohol depresses the immune system and suppresses the ability of our natural killer cells to destroy cancer. These cells are thought to be one of the body's most important defenses against cancer. I don't think a few drinks are worth the risk of possible recurrence of the tumor.

QUESTION: My 21-year-old son is normally a quiet and friendly person who has never been in any trouble. Until this past year, he did not drink any alcohol, but when he started to drink he got into trouble every time. Even though he and his friends tell me that he only has one or two drinks, my son becomes violent, gets into fights, and really scares people. He says he won't drink again because two weeks ago it took police to control him. Is alcohol the cause of this change in behavior?

ANSWER: Your son probably has a relatively rare condition known as pathological intoxication, whereby alcohol acts paradoxically in that it excites rather than sedates. Ordinarily, people affected by this disorder exhibit marked aggressiveness with assaultive and destructive behavior after drinking only a small amount of alcohol. Hostility, rage, and violent outbursts toward others, with no memory of what happened, are also consistent with the diagnosis of pathological intoxication. The only treatment is absolute abstinence from alcohol.

Question: I get abdominal pain when I drink alcohol. It happens almost every time I drink. The doctor in the emergency room said that I probably have pancreatitis. What is pancreatitis?

Answer: The pancreas is a gland in the upper part of the abdomen behind the stomach. It produces digestive enzymes along with the hormone insulin. Acute attacks of upper abdominal pain from pancreatitis that follow drinking alcohol can become progressively more severe and have a mortality rate of up to 30 percent. The condition may become chronic with insufficient digestive enzyme production, reduced insulin production, and the development of diabetes mellitus. Treatment, of course, is to abstain from alcohol.

Question: Besides liver and brain damage, are there any other physical consequences of heavy drinking?

Answer: These two should be enough, but usually, even before these two develop, there is a litany of common disorders that may appear with chronic alcohol consumption: Dupuytren's contracture, a contraction of the tendons in the forearm; aseptic necrosis of the hips, a disruption of the blood supply to the head of the femur bone; high blood pressure; holiday heart, or atrial fibrillation, a marked irregularity of the heartbeat; dangerously lowered potassium levels if one is taking diuretics; pathological changes in the stomach lining that take twenty-four months to heal; pancreatitis (75 percent of cases are related to chronic drinking); and severe diarrhea associated with folic acid deficiency. Most of these are treated as primary conditions but in reality they are frequently alcohol related.

QUESTION: My friend of twenty years (she is 55) has been a chronic alcoholic for at least thirty-five years of her life. She also indulges in snorting speed and uses various other drugs, some prescribed, some not. About six months ago, her retina detached in the left eye and now her right eye is in jeopardy with tears, or rips, in the retina. My question is this: Are all these years of nonstop alcohol and drug abuse, along with daily doses of tamoxifen, the cause of her current eye problems?

ANSWER: I presume your friend is under the care of an ophthalmologist. Chronic alcohol consumption, extending to many years, often causes an eye condition called toxic amblyopia characterized by a loss of visual acuity in both eyes. Paralysis of the muscles that control movement of the eyeball is another consequence of long-term drinking, and both oculomotor palsy and toxic amblyopia are probably linked to the malnutrition of chronic alcoholism associated with thiamine (vitamin B₁) deficiency. Neither tamoxifen, a breast cancer treatment drug, nor amphetamines and other forms of "speed" have been reported to cause retinal detachment. Has your friend ever considered alcohol treatment? It appears from her history that there is an urgency to intervene in the alcohol problem.

QUESTION: I have been in recovery with A.A. for three and a half years; I am also anorexic. Is there a connection between alcoholism and anorexia and bulimia?

ANSWER: There is evidence of a relationship between eating disorders and alcohol abuse in women. A study (Goldbloom. *British Journal of Addiction* 87, 1992) of two populations of adult women, those presenting for alcoholism treatment and those referred to a specialized eating disorder program, showed that 30 percent of the women in alcoholism treatment met the diagnostic criteria for an eating disorder, and 26.9 percent of the women in the eating disorder program met the criteria for alcohol dependence. These rates exceed the general population norms. However, the basis for coprevalence is unknown and each condition requires a different form of treatment. I would say that you should approach your physician and be treated for anorexia since you're already in A.A. It's also very important that you tell your physician about your history of drinking and your recovery program.

QUESTION: My physician advised me to stop drinking because of gastritis. Does drinking cause gastritis?

ANSWER: Yes, and as the thoroughness of your physician has shown, your gastritis is almost certainly the result of your drinking. Gastritis is an inflammation of the lining of the stomach and is most commonly caused by the astringent irritation of alcohol. This inflammation is associated with bleeding from the lining's surface, with the amount of bleeding varying from minimal but constant to gross blood loss. The treatment, of course, is to stop drinking. The changes in the stomach lining can take up to six months or more to return to normal. Drinking to the extent that you have developed gastritis suggests you may need some help in stopping drinking and, more important, staying stopped. Consider calling A.A.

QUESTION: Can four to five drinks a day cause anemia?

ANSWER: Yes, if this goes on for a long time. Alcohol is thought to inhibit the use of iron by the bone marrow in the manufacture of red blood cells. Also, chronic alcohol abuse is commonly associated with gastrointestinal bleeding, in which iron is lost and not available for recycling in the making of new red cells. A poor diet, not uncommon in chronic alcohol dependence, may make the iron intake insufficient. The result is iron deficiency anemia. Also, alcohol interferes with the absorption of vitamin B_{12} and folate in the small intestine, both of which are essential to the production of red blood cells. Chronic alcohol use also impairs other blood functions, including the ability of white cells to defend the body against infections and the bone marrow production of platelets, which plays a major role in normal clotting and wound repair.

QUESTION: Recently, I was driving to work at 6:30 A.M. when I was stopped and arrested for drunk driving. The police said that my blood alcohol was above the legal limit. The night before I had been at a late party where I had a lot to drink, but my last drink was at about 2:30 A.M. I slept for a few hours, got up, ate something, and drove to work. Could I still have that much alcohol in me?

ANSWER: You can, and this is how that happens. Let's presume that your "lot to drink" came to ten or more drinks over a period of four hours. Since the body metabolizes alcohol at the rate of one drink per hour, by 6:30 A.M. when you were driving to work your blood alcohol would be in the range of 0.1 percent, well above the legal limit; not until about noon would your blood alcohol level be at the 0 level. The fact that you slept and then ate between the party and driving to work has no effect on the rate at which your body metabolizes and excretes the alcohol.

QUESTION: Does drinking have any special bad effects on an insulin-dependent diabetic?

ANSWER: In addition to all the other organ damage that can happen to anyone who drinks large amounts of alcohol over a period of time, diabetics have a very dangerous condition to be concerned about. If a diabetic drinks heavily and at the same time doesn't eat, the natural glycogen stores, or sugar reserve, in the liver will be depleted. If a diabetic then takes his usual dose of insulin, thus reducing an already low blood sugar level, he can lapse into a profound or even fatal coma. This condition is called alcoholic hypoglycemia. Diabetics who drink alcohol must maintain their liver glycogen stores by eating regularly because alcohol retards glycogen formation.

QUESTION: Over the past few months I have pains in my stomach after a few drinks, which continue for a couple of hours. When I don't drink alcoholic beverages, I don't have any trouble. I have been a fairly heavy drinker for years, but I don't think of it as a problem. Now I know that if I take even two drinks I get these pains. What's happening?

Answer: Your body may be warning you that your heavy drinking days may be nearing an end. It is possible, even probable, that each time you drink alcohol, these same distressing symptoms will occur. Your pain can come from several conditions. The most likely cause is alcoholic gastritis, an inflammation of the stomach lining caused by alcohol. The symptoms include nausea, vomiting, and some bleeding. This inflammation heals over a three-month period with abstinence. Another, more uncommon, condition is pancreatitis, an inflammation of the gland that lies in the upper abdomen and produces vital substances for your body such as insulin.

It seems, regardless of the cause, that once these symptoms of upper abdominal pain begin to occur after drinking, they will continue each time a person drinks. Alcoholic pancreatitis can progress from repeated acute attacks following alcohol intake to a more chronically debilitating condition called chronic relapsing pancreatitis. Alcohol causes one third of all pancreatitis cases. Gallstones cause another third, and other conditions, viral, drug-induced, metabolic, or traumatic, cause the remaining third. Most people in whom this condition exists should stop drinking permanently, simply because they cannot tolerate the effects of "just a few drinks."

Call your physician now to schedule an appointment and find out what condition you are suffering from. There are other disorders not related to alcohol that can cause these symptoms as well.

QUESTION: I had a hemorrhage from my varicose veins in the esophagus. My physician tells me that this rupture of blood vessels is linked to alcoholic cirrhosis of the liver. Do people recover from this?

ANSWER: Your doctor has no doubt told you that since you survived the hemorrhage from the esophageal varices, the most important thing in your life from here on in is abstinence from alcohol. If you continue drinking, you will eventually die from the complications of liver disease. However, you have a pretty good chance of long-term survival if you follow your doctor's orders. I recommend strongly that you call Alcoholics Anonymous, where you will get all the help you need to stay sober and may even meet a few more survivors of esophageal hemorrhage.

QUESTION: Is there a connection between breast cancer and alcohol?

ANSWER: There seems to be. A recent statistical analysis of a number of studies (*Alcohol Health and Research World* 16 (3): 223–229, 1992) suggests that breast cancer rates tend to increase proportionately with increasing exposure to alcohol. The average increase in risk of breast cancer associated with each drink consumed daily is about 10 percent—so if you have two drinks each day over a long period of time, your chances of getting breast cancer will increase 20 percent. Experiments show that after three months women who drink daily will have increased levels of serum estrogen at about the time of ovulation. Because increased levels of estrogen have been implicated as a cause of breast cancer in humans, this alcohol–hormone link fits with existing theories of the mechanism of breast cancer in humans.

QUESTION: Does having a couple of drinks a day prevent heart attacks?

ANSWER: Controversy surrounds the findings that drinkers of "moderate amounts" of alcohol, usually defined as one to two drinks a day, experience lower rates of death from cardiovascular disease than heavy drinkers or nondrinkers. This possible preventive effect of two drinks is related to an increase of high-density lipoprotein (HDL), and evidence suggests that the level of this cholesterol is inversely related to coronary artery heart disease (Farchi, G., et al. Alcohol and Mortality in the Italian Rural Cohorts of the Seven Countries Study. *International Journal of Epidemiology* 21 (1): 74–81, 1992). Although one dimension of health may seem to be improved by a small amount of alcohol per day, other dimensions may be worsened. For example, one study showed that one drink a day lowered the risk of heart attack, but it increased the risk of hemorrhagic stroke in women. Another study showed that women who drank one-half drink a day experienced a 30 percent increase in relative risk of breast cancer, while those who drank more than one drink increased the relative risk of breast cancer by 50 percent (Stamfer, M.J., et al. A Perspective Study of Moderate Alcohol Consumption and the Risk of Coronary Disease and Stroke in Women. *New England Journal of Medicine* 319 (5): 267–273). In any case, alcohol, in any amount, would not be prescribed as a preventive measure for coronary heart disease and would be absolutely prohibited for any person recovering from alcoholism.

QUESTION: Does drinking beer cause one to put on weight?

ANSWER: Yes, but so does drinking any other kind of alcoholic beverage. Studies show that alcohol slows the rate at which the body burns fat by at least one third. Anyone who makes his or her way through a six-pack a day probably shifts metabolism so that fat, which would ordinarily be broken down and sent out of the body, will likely end up on the hips, thighs, or abdomen. But, as someone said, "it's the alcohol in the beer that adds the flab."

Question: Does LSD have any bad effects on the body?

Answer: No, but it sure has a bad effect on thinking. To make matters riskier, we have no clear idea of why dropping acid acts on the mind the way it does. The bizarre mental responses to this very potent drug tell us that it works on the highest level of brain function. The certainty of LSD users who experience intense revelations or insight that makes little sense to anyone else besides LSD users suggests that the user is playing around with a kind of insanity. Users also claim an increase in the awareness of profound philosophical breakthroughs. However, there are reports of permanent mental impairment resulting from use of this drug. Flashbacks, spontaneous returns to a state of mind similar to the LSD trip without the aid of any drug, are a clue to the possible permanency of the drug's effect. Although LSD does not produce a physical dependency with continued use, psychological dependence appears to develop, and deaths have occurred during LSD trips as the result of irrational behavior induced by the drug.

Question: I am a 32-year-old Asian man and I drink about three or four beers a day, after which my face becomes neon red and also burns. What is the cause? Please, is there anything short of not drinking—period—that can be done?

ANSWER: "Not drinking—period" is the way to avoid having a neon-red face after a few beers, or any other kind of alcoholic beverage for that matter. People who flush and whose skin on the face burns after a beer or so lack a certain enzyme in the liver required to metabolize, or break down, alcohol completely. Normally, alcohol passes through the mouth, then to the stomach and intestine, and then to the liver. The liver metabolizes alcohol at the rate of one drink per hour, no faster, no slower. This process involves turning alcohol into another chemical called acetaldehyde, which is immediately broken down to other simple substances the body eliminates. In some people, including most Asian people, there is a lack of the enzyme needed to complete this series of chemical reactions in the liver, and the acetaldehyde circulates in the body, causing all kinds of unpleasant feelings.

There is a drug, disulfiram, which produces this negative reaction and is given to people who are trying to refrain from drinking entirely. If a person who is taking the pill regularly has a drink, then he or she will develop a neon face, burning skin, and frequently heart palpitations that are pretty scary.

Incidentally, there is nothing known at this time that can be done to change the way your liver metabolizes alcohol, and that being the case, drinking is just not worth it. Also, I must add, it's normal not to need to drink.

QUESTION: Can alcohol cause problems with sexual function?

ANSWER: Yes, it can. Alcohol has a direct and indirect damaging effect on testicular, or male sex gland, tissue. As a result of a man's long-term alcohol abuse, the amount of male sex hormone in his body decreases so that he becomes impotent and his sex glands produce greatly reduced numbers of sperm, a condition known as relative sterility. Furthermore, with reduced circulating testosterone, long-term alcohol abuse can lead to feminizing features in men, such as loss of facial and body hair, female breast configuration, and reduced muscle mass, due to a relative increase in estrogenic (female) hormones in the liver. Even short-term, heavy use of alcohol temporarily lowers male sex hormone levels, but long-term, heavy drinking causes irreversible damage.

In the female, heavy alcohol use during pregnancy can have a profound adverse effect on the development of the fetus. Alcohol can also interfere with ovarian function, causing a disruption in the normal female cycle. So, yes, alcohol interferes with the delicate biochemical and hormonal functioning of the sexual system, and continued long-term, heavy drinking can shut the system down permanently.

QUESTION: What effect does eating have on alcohol consumption?

ANSWER: Drinking alcohol on an empty stomach will heighten the alcohol blood level within the first hour of drinking or less. If a person drinks the same amount one to two hours after an average meal, the blood alcohol level peaks much more slowly and never reaches the same level as after drinking on an empty stomach. With food in the stomach, the body has a slower rate of absorption of alcohol. Specifically, fatty foods block absorption of alcohol longer than protein or carbohydrate foods because they take longer to digest. Essentially, it is not advisable to drink alcohol on an empty stomach because the alcohol is absorbed into the bloodstream that much more quickly and has that much more potent an effect on the brain.

QUESTION: I enjoy skiing and do it a lot. What is the effect of alcohol in conditions of extreme cold?

ANSWER: Alcohol has an undeserved popular reputation of being a useful substance to warm people up in a cold environment. Just the reverse is true. Alcohol does increase cutaneous blood flow, or circulation of blood to the area closest to our skin, but while this makes a person feel warmer, it actually accelerates heat loss from the body. There is also evidence that alcohol in large doses can impair the body's thermal regulatory center, making it difficult for the brain to signal when the body is approaching hypothermia. Without a doubt, drinking when one is exposed to severe cold is dangerous. The faithful St. Bernard dog with the cask of brandy attached to its collar may have been a welcome sight to those lost, but he also might have made things worse for the lost wayfarer on the frigid alpine slopes.

QUESTION: I'm 22 years old and have always had trouble with my weight. When I stick to a strict diet, my weight will go down but I find myself drinking more. In fact, my drinking is causing me to have the same poor image of myself as I had when I was much heavier. Is there some connection between drinking and dieting?

ANSWER: It seems that there is. Within the past twenty years, researchers have found that patients with eating disorders, especially bulimia, often suffer from alcohol abuse or dependence. Studies show that the more severe the degree of dieting, the more frequent the use of alcohol. The severity of dieting is correlated not only to the frequency of alcohol use, but also with the frequency of blackouts and other negative outcomes of heavy drinking. So what has long been suspected is now being clarified by research; there is a connection between eating disorders with severe dieting and alcohol abuse or dependence (*Psychiatric Times,* 2/93).

AGE AND GENDER

ALCOHOLISM AND OTHER drug dependencies cross all boundaries of age and gender, and as we sort through the general population, different issues come up with different groups of people. For instance, studies show that the incidence of alcoholism peaks at age 45, then drops off, only to peak again in the sixties. There seem to be more alcoholic men than women. Young people who abuse drugs tend to use a variety of drugs plus alcohol. Elderly addicted people are more inclined to use only alcohol, but many elderly also abuse prescription drugs. It's therefore useful to keep in mind the specific physical, mental, and emotional situations and tendencies of individuals.

THE ELDERLY

QUESTION: I am 68 years old and for years I have enjoyed a glass or two of wine at dinner, but throughout the past six months it seems the wine has a much stronger effect than it did before. Does my age have anything to do with it?

ANSWER: Your age has probably the most to do with this increased sensitivity to alcohol. As one gets older, and especially after one reaches 65, there is a decrease in lean body mass and hence in body water content. This means that for a given quantity of alcohol, there is a higher blood alcohol concentration in your system at this age than when you were younger. In addition, your slower metabolism at this time of life accounts for substantially higher blood alcohol concentrations. One other factor must be considered. If you are taking any medication, the way your body handles alcohol with other drugs, especially sedatives or tranquilizers, could greatly increase your response to alcohol. But, because of your aging brain's increased sensitivity to alcohol and increased blood alcohol concentration due to slower metabolism and an increased ratio of body fat to water, even as little as three drinks a day can impair your functioning.

QUESTION: My father is 67 years old, and during the past year he has been getting more forgetful and seems to be going through a personality change. He blows up at the slightest thing and is irritable much of the time. He always has been a very friendly, outgoing person, but now all he wants is to be left alone. He says we're all plotting to put him in a nursing home. We finally got him to go to the doctor on the pretext that at his age he should at least have an annual checkup. The doctor said that his liver was somewhat enlarged, but otherwise he was in pretty good physical condition. My father denied ever drinking heavily and said that he now has only a glass of wine occasionally. The doctor explained to us, my mother and sister and I, that this change in behavior strongly suggests the onset of Alzheimer's disease. When we told the doctor that my father drinks from 4 to 6 ounces of bourbon a day, he commented that this might explain the enlarged liver but that small amount couldn't account for the behavior change. Please give us your opinion on this.

ANSWER: Four ounces of whiskey daily adds up to a fifth of whiskey every six days. This is a lot of alcohol for a 67-year-old man. Elderly people lose their tolerance to alcohol, so that much smaller amounts cause brain damage. Up to 10 percent of those persons over the age of 60 who are diagnosed as having Alzheimer's disease are actually suffering from the effects of alcohol consumption according to one study (Iber, F.L.: University of Maryland). Furthermore, the symptoms of Alzheimer's disease are indistinguishable from the symptoms of chronic heavy drinking in some elderly. The huge difference in the two conditions is that the brain damage in chronic alcohol consumption is often reversible, whereas the brain damage in Alzheimer's is not.

To find out what is really happening to your father, get him to stop drinking any alcohol permanently. This may require all the skills and persuasion you have, but it will be worth it. Dr. Iber's study shows that it takes about two months of abstention from alcohol for the brain of the elderly drinker to clear. I would consider this an urgent task for your family, because if your father continues to drink, irreversible brain damage can eventually occur from the alcohol. Incidentally, when your father stops drinking, his liver condition will improve as well. I must also urge you to include a treatment plan in your intervention efforts. Your father will need all the resources he has to maintain abstinence and treatment, possibly beginning with detoxification.

QUESTION: Does taking vitamins prevent damage to a person who is still drinking almost daily? My father insists that because he has been taking vitamins, drinking hasn't hurt him a bit. He is 72 and gets drunk at least twice a week on much less than he used to drink.

ANSWER: Lots of things are happening to your father. First of all, absorption of vitamins is impaired in chronic alcohol consumers. The harmful effect of alcohol on that

72-year-old brain far exceeds the benefit of any vitamin. One vitamin, B_1, is so essential to brain function that its absence causes the most common serious, chronic brain disorder—the Wernicke-Korsakoff syndrome. Occasionally, large infusions of vitamin B_1 may restore brain function, including memory, orientation, abstract thinking, and concentration, in the Korsakoff disorder, but neither prevention nor treatment will work if a person is still drinking.

By the way, 72 is not too old to recover, but if your father continues to drink, he is at risk of progressing to an alcoholic dementia, which is often indistinguishable from Alzheimer's disease.

QUESTION: According to my mother, my grandmother drank nothing until two years ago. She is 66 years old and is a very prim and elegant lady. Lately she has alcohol on her breath most of the time and occasionally slurs her speech. She denies outright that she has been drinking. Yesterday she fell, but luckily she did not hurt herself. Is it possible that she is an alcoholic even though she didn't start to drink until two years ago?

ANSWER: Yes, it is possible and even very likely that she is one of the elderly late-onset alcoholics who are becoming more frequently identified as we learn more about this disease. First, she is exhibiting the common distortion of thinking by denying that she even drinks. Also, because she is older, her tolerance of alcohol is less than that of a younger woman, and a small amount of alcohol goes a long way. Likewise, her metabolism has slowed down so the effect of each drink will last longer. Because of these physiological characteristics, an older person drinking as little as three glasses of wine a day could qualify as an alcoholic. If her denial appears to be impenetrable, it would be wise to organize a formal intervention and get her into treatment before she falls again and breaks her hip. As you probably know, falls are the second most common cause of alcohol-related accidental deaths after auto crashes. It has been said, "Behind the closed doors of his home, under the facade of senility or chronic illness, beyond the scrutiny of society, at least one in ten elderly Americans is quietly drinking himself to death" (Champlin, *Geriatric Magazine,* 1983).

QUESTION: I am 67 years old and do not have any problem with alcohol. I don't drink at all, but I am nervous at times and I was thinking of asking my doctor for some mild medicine to take when I feel this way. Could I become addicted to a drug like the one he might prescribe?

ANSWER: Maybe, so don't start! There is a probability that as you continued to take a prescription like this over a period of time for nervousness or anxiety, you would come to depend upon it. Therein lies the rub. My experience with elderly individuals shows that many who use a prescription of this kind find an ever-increasing need to take it until eventually they become not only psychologically but physically dependent upon it. Indeed, one study reports that the elderly take 25 percent of all prescriptions and that 25 percent of these are psychoactive drugs such as anti-anxiety agents (tranquilizers) and sedative–hypnotics (Abrams, R.C., et al. *Hospital Community Psychology* 38: 1285–1287). There are better ways to deal with nervousness than with chemicals. A few are easy exercises like walking and mild aerobics, and joining some fun-related or even therapy-oriented group at a senior center. You could try meditation, which many find soothing. Finally, remember, all of us have to put up with some nervousness at times, and that just learning how to cope with these feelings is a good skill to have.

QUESTION: I am a senior citizen and have arthritis in my hands, feet, and back, but the pain in my hands and feet is the worst. I have found that a couple of drinks are the best painkiller for me. My wife says that there must be some better ways to deal with the pain, but she has always been against drinking anyway. I have tried all the other stuff for arthritis and it doesn't work as well or as fast as a drink or two. I told her I would write to you for your opinion.

ANSWER: Well, your wife is actually right! Alcohol is the absolute worst thing you can take for pain in a chronic disease—or any other disease, for that matter. Since the pain of arthritis is fairly constant, the use of your medicine of choice—alcohol—would necessarily be frequent. Not only that, alcohol is an addictive drug that builds up a tolerance, requiring you to take more of the "pain medicine" to get the same relief. Though alcohol may provide a kind of detachment from the discomfort of the joint pain, it is also toxic to the liver and brain and inevitably leads to liver disease and mental deterioration. I am concerned that your wife is concerned; she is probably observing that your arthritis may be the entry point to a case of alcoholism in a senior citizen. Please take her advice and stop using alcohol as your painkiller.

YOUNG PEOPLE

QUESTION: Is alcohol abuse more common than drug abuse in young people?

ANSWER: Yes. Alcohol abuse/dependence is the most common chronic illness between the ages of 18 and 44; drug abuse/dependence is the second most common.

Question: I am a student body president in a mid-sized college. I would like to start a discussion group about drug and alcohol abuse on campus. Is there some source of information I can get for this?

Answer: Yes, the Center for Substance Abuse Prevention's National Clearinghouse for Alcohol and Drug Information publishes a resource guide about alcohol and college youth (June 1991, currently being revised). This is a free government publication and the telephone number you can call to request a copy is (800) 729-6686. Here are a few of the gems of information in this guide:

- Of the current student body in America, between 2 and 3 percent will eventually die from alcohol-related causes, about the same number as will get advanced degrees, master's and doctor's degrees combined.

- A survey of college administrators showed that they believed that alcohol is a factor in 34 percent of all academic problems and 25 percent of dropout cases.

- There is virtually no college campus in America where drinking is not regulated in some way. Beer is banned on 22 percent of the campuses, and 29 percent do not allow distilled spirits on campus.

- Approximately 35 percent of all college newspaper advertising revenue comes from alcohol advertisement.

QUESTION: What is the children's program in alcohol treatment centers?

ANSWER: It is a three-day education program (followed by a twelve-week aftercare program) for children 6 to 12 years old who are not involved in alcohol or drugs, but who come from an alcoholic or drug-dependent family. The program goals are parent–child communication, education of the child on the disease, trust building, and learning to identify and share feelings. At least one parent must be involved in a recovery program, and at least one parent (either mother or father) must participate in the children's program. Following are sample comments by children after completion of the program:

- "I can't make an alcoholic stop drinking."
- "I wish I could have no alcohol in the world."
- "I play many rolls [sic]."
- "Sharing your feelings is good."
- "I can be an alcoholic threw [sic] my genes."
- "I learned you can die from alcohol and what chemical dependent means and lots more stuff."
- "I wish I were a millionaire and I wish there was no alcohol person in my family and my parents weren't divorced."

Most children of alcoholics grow up in families where the secret of alcoholism is never spoken; they feel that somehow they may be the cause of it. It's a heavy burden for a kid to bear, and it may distort all of his or her future perceptions. This kind of program can be of great help to a child.

QUESTION: My son tells me that all the kids sniff glue and things like that to get a dizzy feeling. He says they only do it for fun. What do you say?

ANSWER: All the kids don't do this, but some do—8 percent of fourth graders were found to have sniffed similar substances in a large study (Cohen, S. Pharmacology of Drugs of Abuse. *Drug Abuse and Alcoholism Newsletter* 5(6): 1, July 1976). Your instinct about the dangers of inhalants is valid. Volatile inhalants that youngsters use, a practice that is called "huffing" among kids, all produce a dizziness and giddiness that is the goal of the experience. Lurking within these vapors, however, are very toxic substances that react immediately with the human nervous system, and there have been some instances in which inhalants have caused death by sudden cardiac arrest. The most common substances children abuse are butane from cigarette lighters, gasoline, paint thinner, freon, and any aerosol product. The Federal Drug Abuse Warning Network reported seventy-six deaths from huffing these inhalants in 1991. By high school, one student in every five has used inhalants at least once. If I were you, I'd share these facts with your son and do what you can to convince him of the very real dangers of inhalants.

QUESTION: I have seen young people with open sores on their bodies that are similar to chicken pox. I was told this was because of long-term use of speed (amphetamines) and if one came in contact with the sores, they could acquire hepatitis B. Is this true and would cocaine do this also?

ANSWER: A person could contact hepatitis B in this case only if the person with the open sores had hepatitis B and if the contacted person had an open wound so that the discharge from the open sores was passed through the open wound into the bloodstream. This transmission sounds very unlikely, if not impossible. Incidentally, chronic cocaine and amphetamine users often have open sores on their arms, legs, and stomach from "skin picking" at subcutaneous "bugs" that don't exist.

QUESTION: I am a high school teacher. I understand that there has been a resurgence of LSD use in young people. Can you comment on this.

Answer: LSD (lysergic acid diethylamide) is a drug developed in the 1940s that became popular among young people in the 1960s. It is called a psychedelic drug because it produces a bizarre set of reactions all the way from those described as a religious mystical experience to terrorizing psychotic breaks from reality. A negative reaction to LSD is commonly referred to as a bad trip. With the usual oral dose, about 100 to 250 mcg (micrograms), the user may experience a rapid heartbeat, increased rate of breathing, and increasing fear. From the first to the sixth hour after taking LSD, frightening visual images that do not exist may appear to the user. Users have been known to develop a toxic psychosis that allows them to be convinced that they can perform feats such as safely walking out a tenth-story window; these thoughts constitute a major, and sometimes fatal, departure from rational thought. Deaths have occurred from users acting on such bizarre notions during this acute LSD intoxication. People who use LSD repeatedly are likely to develop depression that could be sufficiently severe to lead to suicide. They are also subject to flashbacks of vivid and frightening visions, which may last for as long as six months to a year and, in some cases, stretch out into a prolonged psychotic reaction. There is also a real danger that LSD can resurrect a previous psychiatric illness. LSD, like other drugs such as PCP (phencyclidine), strike at the very root of a person's mind. The exact neurological process by which these dire negative effects occur is unknown. I would share this information with your classes so they know the dangers of this drug.

QUESTION: What, if any, are the symptoms and/or signs by which it is possible to identify a person using marijuana? I am a high school teacher and I am suspicious about the wide swings in academic performance in some of my students.

ANSWER: Marijuana is four to five times more potent than it was just twenty years ago, so the signs of its use are usually identifiable (Marijuana Use and Health: Drug and Alcohol Concerns: http://www.Columbia.edu/cu/healthwise/0791.html, Columbia University). The effects of this drug involve the cerebral, cardiovascular, pulmonary, and neuroregulatory systems. Manifestations of acute or chronic use include some, or possibly all, of the following: euphoria, decreased mental functioning, increased pulse rate, decreased pulmonary function, exacerbation of asthma, conjunctival injection (red eyes), pharyngitis (sore throat), bronchitis, stuffy nose, dry mouth, sinusitis, perceptual delusions, paranoid feelings, mood shifts (joy to sorrow, fear to elation), sleepiness, heightened sexual arousal, anxiety to panic, lethargy and lack of ambition (with chronic use), and angina in those with preexisting heart disease. The symptoms of overdose are very rapid pulse, markedly high blood pressure, delusions, hallucinations, seizures in epileptics, and acute mental changes including psychosis. There are withdrawal signs for regular users who quit abruptly: irritability, restlessness, insomnia, mild tremors and bouts of chills, and occasionally a low-grade fever. Perhaps this litany of symptoms will be helpful to you. Children and adolescents who use marijuana are reported to be eighty-five times more likely to use cocaine than those who have never used the substance.

QUESTION: Is there any connection between smoking cigarettes and other drug use in children?

ANSWER: Most definitely! I'm glad you said "other drug" use, because tobacco is a drug. In fact, cigarettes, along with alcohol and marijuana, are considered a "gateway drug." An October 1994 report from the Center on Addiction and Substance Abuse at Columbia University states that there are remarkably consistent relationships between the use of cigarettes and alcohol and the subsequent use of marijuana. This is also true of the use of cigarettes, alcohol, and marijuana and the subsequent use of illicit drugs like cocaine, regardless of the age, sex, ethnicity, or race of the individuals involved. Children 12 to 17 years old who use marijuana are eighty-five times more likely to use cocaine than children who have never used it; children who drink are fifty times more likely, and those who smoke are nineteen times more likely to use cocaine. The report also found that the younger children are when they use these gateway drugs and the more often they use them, the more likely they are to use cocaine, heroin, hallucinogens, and other illicit drugs. Sixty percent of children who smoke pot before the age of 15 move on to cocaine; 20 percent of those who first smoke pot after age 17 use cocaine. The report concludes that the data are already robust enough to make a strong case to step up efforts to prevent childhood use of cigarettes, alcohol, and marijuana, and to take firm steps to reduce children's access to these gateway drugs. It goes without saying that it is illegal for children and teens to use cigarettes and alcohol, as well as illicit drugs.

QUESTION: How can I tell when my 14-year-old son is using drugs? I've heard him say that some of his friends smoke marijuana, but he said he never does. In the past few months he seems to act differently. Is this just a stage of adolescence? I'm worried.

ANSWER: You should watch for some classic signs that can appear when a young person gets into drugs. There may be an abrupt change in your son's mood or attitude, or he might show sudden continuing resistance to discipline at home or at school, a distancing from family members, an unusual flaring of temper, or unusual requests for money or even stealing of money from home or school. He may show a heightened secrecy about his actions and possessions and an association with new friends, especially those who use drugs. Most commonly, the most significant signal of drug or alcohol trouble is a sudden and continuing decline of attendance or performance at school. If you observe evidence of probable drug-influenced change in your son, I would recommend that you take an active parenting role by bringing your concern out in the open with your son and his teachers or counselors. If your concerns are warranted in any way, I believe that setting some firm boundaries is very important.

Question: What real harm could come from getting high on inhalants? I've heard that many kids do it, especially the younger ones.

Answer: Sudden death by way of cardiac arrest (sudden heart stoppage) is the most serious and not uncommon hazard associated with children taking "deep whiffs" of the fluorocarbons contained in aerosols. These chemicals sensitize the heart muscle to the stimulating effects of a naturally occurring substance in our body called epinephrine, leading to a wildly irregular heartbeat, very rapid pulse, and finally, with too many kids, cardiac arrest. There are many household and commercial inhalant products available for misuse; the most common are gasoline, paint thinners, model cements and glues, aerosol sprays, antifreeze, and degreasing/cleaning fluids. The effect for which these substances are sniffed is a "high" consisting of euphoria, excitement, relaxation of all inhibitions, and hallucinations with dizziness and slurred speech. These inhalants pose a very real danger that children should be warned against.

WOMEN AND ALCOHOL

QUESTION: Are there any clues as to whether a woman may become alcoholic?

ANSWER: Alcoholism in the immediate family (genetic) may be an indicator. In general, according to the National Institute of Alcohol Abuse and Alcoholism, a woman's drinking resembles that of her husband, siblings, or close friends. Whereas younger women (age 18 to 34) report higher rates of drinking-related problems than do older women, the incidence of alcohol dependence is greater among middle-aged women (age 35 to 49).

Contrary to popular belief, women who have multiple roles, such as married women who work outside the home, may have lower rates of alcohol problems than women who do not have multiple roles. In fact, the loss of role as wife, mother, or worker may increase a woman's risk for abusing alcohol. Statistically, women who have never married or who are divorced or separated are more likely to drink heavily and experience alcohol-related problems than women who are married or widowed. Unmarried women living with a partner are more likely still to engage in heavy drinking and to develop drinking problems.

Question: Does alcohol have a greater effect on women than it does on men?

Answer: Yes, if you mean "Does a woman get drunker quicker than a man of the same size with the same number of drinks?" There are several reasons for this. When alcohol is consumed, it diffuses uniformly into all body water. Because women have a smaller amount of total body water than men, the alcohol concentration is higher in women. In addition to this, women may have far less or none of the primary enzyme, alcohol dehydrogenase, involved in the metabolism, or breakdown, of alcohol in the stomach so alcohol levels in women are higher when absorbed from their stomachs than in men. Finally, fluctuations in hormone levels during the menstrual cycle may affect the rate of alcohol metabolism, making women more susceptible to elevated blood alcohol concentrations at different points in their cycle.

Question: Is there any safe amount of alcohol a woman can drink while she is pregnant?

Answer: Drinking alcohol during pregnancy causes a cluster of symptoms called fetal alcohol syndrome (FAS). Neither the amount of alcohol nor the frequency of drinking it during pregnancy that will lead to this syndrome has been established, but it is safest to assume that any amount of alcohol probably puts the fetus at risk. Not only do physical abnormalities show up in the baby with FAS, but it is one of the most common causes of mental retardation in the United States. The use of any drug, including alcohol, during pregnancy causes the blood level of the drug to be the same in the fetus as in the mother. Since all the developing structures in the fetus are so much more vulnerable when exposed to these drugs than adult tissues, there is no safe amount for a woman to drink or use when she is pregnant.

QUESTION: Has there been any research done on the effects of heredity on alcoholism in women?

ANSWER: Yes, there are a number of studies (Cloninger, C.R., et al. Inheritance of Alcohol Abuse. *Archives of General Psychiatry* 38: 861–868, 1981) that show that the relationship between heredity and alcoholism in women and men differ. In general, men show a much more powerful vulnerability to the alcoholic traits of their parents than do women. Although women can carry a genetic predisposition to alcoholism, not only is it a weaker predictor than in men, but it has a different pattern of occurrence. A study of the effect of alcoholism in biological parents on the frequency of alcohol abuse in 913 women disclosed that if only the mother abused alcohol, 10.3 percent of the daughters became alcoholic. If just the father abused alcohol, only 3.9 percent of the daughters became alcoholic. When both the mother and the father were alcohol abusers, 9.8 percent of the daughters developed alcoholism. It was also found that if the father was severely alcoholic with early onset alcoholism, the daughters showed not only a low rate of alcoholism but also a high rate of a psychosomatic difficulty called "diversiform somatization disorder," which means that throughout their lives they experience a series of chronic, psychosomatic complaints. Alcoholism in women also appears to be triggered more directly by the environment than by hereditary factors, which have been shown to act more strongly in men.

QUESTION: Does using cocaine during pregnancy have as negative an effect on the baby as drinking alcohol? If a person has been using cocaine, is being three months pregnant too late to quit, or has the baby already been damaged?

ANSWER: Although there is a chance that the baby may be born with some defect, there is a much greater chance the baby will be normal if the mother of the child quits three months into the pregnancy than if she continues using cocaine for the entire nine months.

The National Association for Perinatal Addiction Research and Education reported in 1993 that 11 percent of deliveries, approximately 375,000 babies annually, are affected by substance abuse during pregnancy. An estimated 60 percent of pregnant women who use cocaine receive no prenatal care.

Cocaine use during pregnancy may cause spontaneous miscarriage, growth retardation, and behavioral and neurological abnormalities in the baby. With higher doses and more prolonged use of cocaine by the mother, more severe complications—such as intracerebral hemorrhage (stroke)—may affect the fetus. Specifically, a report (Chasnoff, Ira J., et al. Cocaine Use During Pregnancy. *New England Journal of Medicine* 313: 666–669, September 12, 1985) describes a cluster of symptoms of complications seen in pregnancy and in the newborn. Pregnancy in cocaine-addicted mothers is associated with a high incidence of infection, especially hepatitis and venereal disease with its possible transmission to the fetus. Labor and delivery are accompanied by an increased incidence of abruptio placenta, or separation of the placenta from the uterine wall before birth, and maternal hemorrhage; both events are potentially fatal to infant and mother.

Fetal monitoring during labor in cocaine-using mothers shows a high rate of fetal distress (Chasnoff, Ira, Burns, Kayreen A., and Burns, William. Cocaine Use in Pregnancy: Perinatal Morbidity and Mortality. *Neurotoxicology and Teratology* 9: 291–293, 1987). Two of the cocaine-exposed fetuses who were monitored developed cerebral hemorrhage (stroke) similar to intracerebral damage that occurs in some adults who use cocaine.

A grave complication that can occur in the newborn is sudden infant death syndrome (SIDS). Ten of sixty-six infants exposed to cocaine during pregnancy died from this syndrome. Some of the mothers of these infants also smoked cigarettes or drank alcohol, but the percentage of SIDS in these cocaine-exposed infants was much higher than that of infants whose mothers drank alcohol, used opiods, or smoked cigarettes only. The average age at sudden death for the ten infants was 46 days.

Cocaine is excreted from the adult twenty-four to thirty hours after use. In the infant, cocaine and its metabolites can persist in the urine for up to six days due to the infant's incompletely developed liver function. There is also some evidence that cocaine can also be passed to the infant through breast milk. The best thing the mother you speak of can do for herself and her child is to stop using cocaine immediately.

QUESTION: About alcoholism in women, do they have a tougher time of it than men? I know that women seem to be more reluctant to come forward about a possible problem with alcohol because they feel ashamed, and because of society's double standard that silently exists—men can drink heavily, but women shouldn't. It was certainly harder for me as a mother of four and a teacher to admit that I had a drinking problem and stop drinking. I delayed much longer than I should have before asking for help. But what are the main differences?

ANSWER: Women do seem to be hit harder than men, and death rates are one of the main indicators. Alcoholic women die at about five times the rate of death for nonalcoholic women in the general population. This death rate is higher than the mortality rate for alcoholic men, which is about three times the expected rate of deaths for men in the general population. One study of women alcoholics found that, on average, they lose about fifteen years from their expected life span. However, these excessive mortality rates for alcoholic women refer to those women who continue drinking. Women who have attained abstinence have the same mortality rate as those women in the general population who are not alcoholic, which is encouraging.

QUESTION: Does alcohol have a similarly damaging effect on the nervous system of women as it does in men?

ANSWER: Yes. Alcoholic brain shrinkage, as measured by computed tomographic scans, has been found to be similar in men and women. The only difference is that women develop brain shrinkage with shorter periods of alcohol exposure, which could be attributed to metabolic differences between men and women (Mann, et al. *Alcohol, Clinical and Experimental Research*, 1992).

DRUGS

PRESCRIPTION DRUGS, ILLEGAL DRUGS, and legal drugs with psychoactive side effects all target the brain. Psychoactive drugs have the property of changing mood, and it is this property that makes them addicting in susceptible people. Elderly people are more frequently habitual users of prescription drugs and alcohol, while younger addicted people are more commonly users of illegal drugs and alcohol. The greatest number of addicts in this country, however, are dependent on two legal drugs: alcohol and nicotine.

The drugs of choice tend to change with each generation. As I've stated earlier, the marijuana that the sixties generation first started experimenting with has become much more potent. So while in the sixties the hippies got a little high from smoking weed, today's young people and not-so-young people who are smoking marijuana are experiencing a much more intense and damaging high, leaving them more vulnerable to its addictive consequences. In the eighties, the drug of choice was cocaine and its derivative crack, whereas today, heroin and LSD seem to be having a renewed popularity. In general, the choice of drugs seems to come in waves, depending on availability and a search for a new and interesting high or escape. But it's clear that drugs continue to come in many forms, and that often hidden from public view is unwitting dependence on a variety of potent and dangerous prescription drugs.

PRESCRIPTION DRUGS

QUESTION: I am concerned that if I ever have to go to the hospital I will be given medicine for pain that could set me off on the drug addiction that I have tried, with success, to be freed from, through Narcotics Anonymous. How can I avoid getting the narcotics they give you after an operation?

ANSWER: Tell your doctor that at one time you were addicted to heroin, as you mention in your letter, and that you are concerned about any kind of medicine that might reactivate that addiction. However, there are medical circumstances in which the use of a drug to relieve pain is essential to survival. I am referring to the crushing chest pain that occurs frequently with a heart attack, or the severe pain that may be the normal aftereffect of major surgery. In both of these medical conditions, the use of a powerful pain-relieving drug is essential to prevent the consequences of unrelieved major pain and could be life-saving. For acute surgical trauma, or a few other medical conditions, these drugs have a short-term essential use. The majority of patients who enter the hospital for most surgery are not given these drugs.

Don't worry—just tell your doctor about your concerns. Remember, when one is in the throes of a heart attack, passing a kidney stone, awakening after a major operation, or feeling the agony of extensive bone and tissue injury, all one gets from these drugs is blessed relief and sometimes prevention of shock with vascular collapse and death. You are right to be wary, but in these rare times the risk of taking those drugs is warranted. Your doctor will be able to give you further details—just ask.

QUESTION: I have been nervous for years. My doctor prescribed tranquilizers for me and for a while I felt better, but now they don't help even though I've doubled the dose against my doctor's instructions. Now I find I can't stop taking them because when I stop, I become extremely shaky and sick. Am I addicted?

ANSWER: Yes, you are addicted. You meet the criteria for addiction, which include psychological dependence, increased tolerance, and withdrawal symptoms when you stop taking the drug. You require medical detoxification treatment, which is a scheduled tapering off of the drug over a period of time. In addition, you should also have the psychological therapy that is provided in a qualified chemical dependency treatment center.

QUESTION: I have been taking a prescribed tranquilizer for a long time. I wonder if there are any serious consequences if I just stop using them. Are there?

ANSWER: I can't answer this question fully without the specific name of the tranquilizer, or benzodiazepine, you are taking. The first piece of advice I will give you, however, is that you call the doctor who prescribed it and ask him or her. The condition for which your tranquilizer was prescribed may still exist and it may still be necessary. Or the tranquilizer you are taking may have to be diminished from your system gradually. Generally, discontinuing long-term benzodiazepine use is a medically significant process and calls for a carefully structured, gradual reduction schedule of tapered doses of the tranquilizer. To stop them abruptly may lead you to experience severe withdrawal symptoms consisting of tremulousness, psychomotor agitation, possible hallucinations, delirium, and convulsive seizures. The severity of the withdrawal syndrome is dependent on the dose and the length of time you have used the drug.

Even the symptoms associated with low-dose, long-term use of benzodiazepines, while not dangerous, are distressing, and may last for months. These include anxiety, insomnia, nightmares, and muscle spasms. The tapering-down process may last from two to six weeks or more, depending on the dose and duration of your use. Incidentally, according to one study, 70 percent of tranquilizer-dependent persons currently abuse alcohol, or have a history of alcohol abuse. I add this to alert you to the indirect dangers of prescription drug dependence, though you already seem to have a feel for their inherent risks. Your instinct to become drug-free is a good one—call your doctor and start on that path today.

QUESTION: In order to sleep, my elderly brother has been hooked on Halcion for two years. At first he took one half tablet at bedtime, then one; now he oftens takes two. I have seen a drastic change in him; the most obvious is his loss of short-term memory. I should also add that he is a closet alcoholic. What is the lowdown on Halcion and what are the effects if it is combined with alcohol? I am eagerly looking for an answer.

ANSWER: You describe a person who has a multiple drug abuse problem. I suspect from what you tell me that your brother is an older adult in his fifties, sixties, or seventies. Since his drug use is at a relatively low dosage and his drinking is of the sneaky closet type, his addiction is not flagrant. It is as deadly, nonetheless, because he shows little tolerance to Halcion, which lingers in his brain while he adds to its effect with alcohol.

Short-term memory loss is characteristic of elderly persons taking these low doses of Halcion and alcohol. A younger person might develop a tolerance more dangerously high than two tablets of Halcion at bedtime. But your brother is dependent upon these psychoactive drugs, no matter how low the dose, so he needs treatment. He first needs to detox from his benzodiazepine (Halcion), which may take up to a week or more, then he must get into a rehabilitation program to prevent relapse into the addiction. Incidentally, treatments for both Halcion and alcohol abuse are the same and can run concurrently. I have a hunch you'll have to break through your brother's denial before he'll seek treatment. It's been my experience that closet drinkers tend to think nobody knows about their drinking.

QUESTION: What can you tell me about kudzu?

ANSWER: Kudzu is an imported weed that grows in the South and has recently become a nuisance, and I assume you bring it up in reference to its success as a treatment for alcoholism. Apparently, it has had an effect in experiments on special breeds of hamsters who seem to prefer alcohol over water. Dr. Bert L. Vallee, a researcher at Harvard Medical School, says that kudzu extract "has been widely used in China and Japan for centuries to treat alcoholism. You can buy it in pill form over the counter in Japan and China." The active ingredient in kudzu extract has been identified as daidzin. This was synthesized and injected into the alcohol-preferring animals, who, as a result, immediately cut their alcohol consumption by at least 50 percent. Another extract from kudzu, daidzein, had a similar effect. So kudzu, which appears to reduce alcohol craving in lab animals, may become a helpful aid after safety and effectiveness have been established for use in humans.

ILLEGAL DRUGS

QUESTION: What does drug use have to do with hepatitis? My friend says she got it from shooting heroin.

ANSWER: It wasn't the heroin that gave her hepatitis; it was shooting the heroin. Of those heroin addicts who mainline, or inject their drugs intravenously with a needle, about 80 percent have hepatitis B and at least 50 percent also contract hepatitis C. There is a virtual epidemic of this viral liver infection among IV drug users. The disease is spread when users share contaminated needles or syringes. Some who become infected progress to full-blown chronic active hepatitis with eventual cirrhosis, while others develop a chronic carrier state that makes one prone to cancer of the liver. Most, however, will recover from the condition if they stop reinfecting themselves with dirty needles.

There is another infection commonly transmitted in the same way, among the same population—AIDS! So, while heroin is a dangerous substance in and of itself, you can see that the risks associated with its use are many, and all of them are potentially lethal.

QUESTION: Does marijuana have any medicinal use?

ANSWER: In a report to the U.S. Congress in 1980, the Secretary of Health, Education and Welfare summarized the research on the therapeutic applications of marijuana. He concluded that while this substance showed definite promise in treating the nausea and vomiting that often accompany cancer chemotherapy, it has not proved invariably superior to other medications. Trials of the active ingredient of marijuana to reduce pressure in open-angle glaucoma produced varied results when used in combination with standard drugs. These therapeutic uses have been suggested for components of the hemp (marijuana) plant, but are not considered accepted or approved as standard treatment.

JAMES W. WEST

QUESTION: What is the rationale behind switching heroin addicts from heroin to methadone?

ANSWER: There are several reasons behind methadone use in the treatment of opiate addiction. Detoxification and replacement of heroin or morphine is the initial reason. In some people who have used heroin for long periods of time, the brain adapts to the drug and becomes tolerant of high opiate doses. When this happens, unless doses of the drug are continued, an intense, almost unbearable craving for the drug occurs. In some opiate addicts, this physiological brain state becomes fixed, and no matter how long one is free of the opiate—months or longer—the craving persists. An adequate daily oral dose of methadone at a legalized methadone clinic abolishes the craving, while the sedative and other narcotic effects of the medication disappear. If the treatment schedule is managed correctly, a methadone maintenance patient will be a normally functioning, alert, and healthy person. Methadone maintenance can be short-term (a few months) or long-term (twenty years or more) and permits the former addict to live a normal life. This method of replacement therapy has been used successfully to treat hundreds of thousands of people, and has been especially effective in moving people out of the criminal cycle of dealing with illegal drug pushers.

QUESTION: Can a person get liver damage from using cocaine?

ANSWER: Yes. When the body deals with a chemical introduced by whatever manner (orally, nasally, or as an inhalant), a chemical process begins by which the body tries to break it down, use it for nourishment, detoxify it, and excrete it. When a person takes cocaine into the body, the main organ for metabolizing it is the liver. A number of chemical reactions occur, one of which includes converting cocaine to norcocaine nitroxide, a by-product of cocaine metabolism that is very toxic to liver tissue. Fortunately, this reaction produces only minimal amounts of this toxic substance with the average cocaine use. However, when one drinks alcohol and uses cocaine at the same time, there is a much greater production of this very toxic cocaine by-product with a commensurate increase in liver damage. In animal studies, when mice were given alcohol (0.15 percent for six days), there were no deaths; when mice were treated with cocaine for six days, there were no deaths; but when the alcohol-treated mice were given one small dose of cocaine, 30 percent died from acute liver damage. We in the field have interpreted these findings to be similar to what happens in the human liver during the alcohol–cocaine metabolic interaction.

Question: How long does craving for cocaine last? I stopped smoking crack fifteen days ago.

Answer: Smoking cocaine delivers the greatest dose the fastest and therefore produces the greatest desire for the drug when you stop using it. Craving is very intense the first four to five days after you stop and then it continues along at various lower levels of intensity for about two weeks beyond that. You might still feel a desire to use the drug after that period, but your nervous system adjusts to the absence of cocaine. The intensity of the craving after snorting cocaine is somewhat less.

However, the cocaine residues in the circuits of the brain, the vivid memory of the cocaine high, and craving can be activated in most recovering addicts by cues such as seeing drug paraphernalia or powdered sugar or sweetener. Just seeing these things, or hearing accounts of cocaine use, or passing through a neighborhood where cocaine was purchased can start your compulsion to use the drug again. Treatment for cocaine dependence includes dealing with these cues or triggers to the more intense cravings you might have. Just how long these reminders will fire up a desire in you to use cocaine I cannot say with accuracy, but this phenomenon is much more vivid in the recovering cocaine addict than in persons dependent on any other drug (alcohol, etc).

There is good news—cocaine addicts have a high chance of complete recovery with treatment. Good luck to you.

QUESTION: Does smoking cocaine cause convulsions? A friend of mine had a fit when he smoked some crack. The doctors in the emergency room said it was the cocaine.

ANSWER: It probably was! Cocaine can, and does, cause convulsions, especially in those who smoke the drug or those who have epilepsy. However, there are some who may experience a seizure without having any history of seizure disorder.

Some people have ingested condoms filled with cocaine in order to transport the drug from one place to another. This is also a very dangerous practice. If the condom breaks and the person ingests a large amount of cocaine, he or she could have an agonal seizure (a predeath convulsion) when the drug is released into the intestine.

QUESTION: Is cocaine use associated with violence?

ANSWER: A study reported in *The Journal of the American Medical Association,* July 6, 1994, showed that homicide victims who used cocaine within two days of their death represent the group that uses ten to fifty times more cocaine than is used by the general population. The report reads that "homicide victims may have provoked violence through irritability, paranoid thinking, or verbal or physical aggression, which are known to be pharmacological effects of cocaine. In addition, homicide may have been part of the business of dealing cocaine." Both cocaine and amphetamines, which have a similar pharmacological action but are not identical, lead to paranoid thinking with heavy use. This in turn can, and often does, lead to violence.

QUESTION: Is marijuana still as popular as it was several years ago? Is it as common a drug of abuse among grade school and high school kids as it used to be?

ANSWER: Over the past three years, the use of marijuana has nearly doubled. According to the American Council for Drug Education in 1993, on an average day, 39,109 pounds of marijuana were brought into the United States, and 3,911 pounds were seized by the Drug Enforcement Administration (DEA). And a 1995 study indicates that there is heavy and growing use of marijuana among grade school, high school, and college students, as well as among adult workers (Leshner, Alan I. *National Institute of Drug Abuse Notes* 10 (4): July–August, 1995).

QUESTION: What is PCP? Is it dangerous?

ANSWER: Phencyclidine, commonly known as PCP, is probably the worst and most dangerous of illegal drugs. The goal of users is to achieve a sensory-deprived trance state. One great danger in the use of this drug lies in the fact that the difference in doses that cause increasingly severe reactions from trance to convulsions to coma is small. There are four stages of PCP's effects that usually occur sequentially: first, there is acute toxicity marked by combativeness, visual illusions, and auditory hallucinations; second, there is a toxic psychosis during which a person may injure himself or others; third, there is severe paranoia and delusions of superhuman strength and invulnerability; and finally, the fourth stage is marked by depression and a very high risk of suicide. This last stage may last from one day to many months. Frequently, users in this stage are brought to hospitals in a wildly uncontrollable state and require restraint to prevent injury to themselves or others. PCP was used in veterinary medicine as an anesthetic but was withdrawn from use due to severe adverse side effects. To repeat, PCP (phencyclidine) has and deserves the worst reputation of all the drugs of abuse.

QUESTION: My son has a good job but has never reached the level of his potential. I visited him recently and he admitted that he still uses marijuana. I know that if he was suspected of using this junk his job would be in jeopardy. When I mention anything about this he goes into a harangue about how drugs should be legalized, and that alcohol should be outlawed. I think it is a mistake to call drugs recreational, as he does. Calling them things like pot or grass seems to say that people are just being naughty by using them. I can't believe they are not addicting. What can you tell me about the effects of marijuana?

ANSWER: Marijuana is addicting, and a lot of other things too. First of all, long-term users report that it is four or five times as potent as it was in the sixties when the flower children gave the impression that using it was a benign kind of hippie thing to do so that one could feel relaxed and euphoric, be aroused sexually, and sometimes experience vivid visual imagery. After smoking, one can also experience an altered perception of time, in which moments seem to pass more slowly. Those with the susceptibility for addictive disease can easily become dependent on marijuana. Marijuana, or pot, has been thought of as a "soft drug" as compared to the "hard drugs" like heroin and cocaine, but research shows that marijuana contains psychoactive substances that react rapidly in the brain and have strong effects on the human cardiovascular, pulmonary, and neuro-regulatory systems that make such a name misleading.

The target organ for marijuana is the brain, where

its active ingredients accumulate. Because marijuana is absorbed into the brain cell wall, it is considered more destructive to brain tissue than the opioids. Heavy use of this drug impairs general intellectual functioning such as memory and comprehension, and even so-called casual use impairs psychomotor skills like those necessary for driving a car.

Three other systems are also affected. First, the respiratory system shows irritation and some obstruction to the smaller airways with a form of bronchitis–emphysema. Marijuana contains four to five times the lung-cancer-producing hydrocarbons as does tobacco. Second, the heart responds to marijuana by an increased heart rate that is proportional to the dose of the drug. Usually, after one smokes pot, the heart rate will increase by 20 to 40 beats per minute, and rapid rates of 140 beats per minute are not unusual. Third, abnormalities can occur in the reproductive systems of both men and women. Marijuana can cause irregularities in the menstrual cycle, and studies of males have shown a reduction in sperm count and motility of the sperm, as well as sperm of abnormal appearance, after marijuana use. Sterility and infertility have occurred in a significant number of users (Hembree, W.C. III. Changes in Human Spermatozoa Associated with High Dose Marijuana Smoking, in Nahas, G., and Paton, W. (eds.). *Marijuana: Biological Effects.* New York: Pergamon Press, 1979). Finally, smoking marijuana during pregnancy has been found to be linked to a form of leukemia in infants.

Question: Does cocaine damage the brain? If so, does it recover?

Answer: Whether cocaine damage to the brain is reversible or not, treatment of any current cocaine use, including total abstinence, is essential. A group from the Department of Radiology at Harvard Medical School reported in the *Journal of Nuclear Medicine* in June 1991 that a group of cocaine-dependent, polydrug users showed defects in brain tissue. The brain scan findings in the cocaine-dependent persons were measured against the findings in a similar number of non–drug-using persons.

The study showed that there is a danger that some cocaine-dependent people will suffer catastrophic hemorrhage within the brain from a sudden increase in blood pressure when they use cocaine. What was not known at the time of this study was the presence and extent of the damage to brain tissue among those cocaine-dependent polydrug users who did not exhibit identifiable symptoms of brain injury.

Single photon emission profusion brain scans revealed that defects exist in several specific regions of the brain of cocaine-dependent polydrug users. These defects are due to a complete or partial shutdown of the blood supply to scattered areas of the brain, more frequently in the frontal and temporal lobes. These scans were done on cocaine users who, in some cases, used other drugs, including alcohol, occasionally or frequently. Some in the study had not used cocaine for one to five years before the scan; others had used it only days before the scan. Doses of cocaine ranged from mild, four times a year by nasal inhalation, to heavy, daily nasal inhalation, IV, and smoking use. The results of this study reveal that defects show up in the brain scan of all users, including those participants who had not used cocaine for some time before the scan. Repeat scans on a number of the recent users revealed that there is about a 25 percent improvement after a one-month abstinence from cocaine. However, those who have abstained for longer periods of time still showed defects. One must conclude from these findings that some brain damage, even with relatively mild cocaine use, occurs, and that this damage could very well be permanent. The defects consist of focal areas of the brain that don't function due to having suffered from diminished blood supply. One can visualize this as a block of Swiss cheese, where cheese is functioning brain and the holes are brain that's lost to function.

Psychometric tests that measure intelligence were done on all subjects in the study and were found to be abnormal. However, in spite of these grave findings, treatment to prevent further damage and possibly lead to improved functioning is imperative for these cocaine users.

Question: What kind of a drug is Ecstasy? I understand that it is used in psychotherapy.

Answer: There is no beneficial use for this drug, technically known as MDMA. Ecstasy is a stimulating hallucinogen that shares some features with mescaline and LSD. According to a report by Marc A. Schuckit, M.D., in his regular newsletter *Drug Abuse and Alcoholism,* "There are data indicating the probability that it causes brain chemical alterations that can last six months or longer after repeated use." In fact, there is considerable danger of an overdose because the minimal lethal dose is so close to the amount necessary to get high.

Question: What is it about cocaine that makes people hooked on it do just about anything to get it?

Answer: Your question pretty well defines what addiction is. Cocaine produces a sense of well-being, exhilaration, self-confidence, and strength; it banishes hunger and fatigue and stimulates a race of euphoric thoughts. It does this by modifying and enhancing naturally occurring neurotransmitters in the brain. People enjoy this feeling so much and their bodies crave a repeat of it so intensely that some will put themselves in a lot of danger to experience it again and again. Large doses of cocaine place the user at risk of death by way of convulsive seizure activity, cardiac arrhythmia, respiratory failure, and asphyxia.

Twenty-two million Americans—one in ten—report they have tried cocaine at least once. Every day, according to Dr. Mark Gold of the University of Florida, about five thousand teenagers and adults try cocaine for the first time. Emergency rooms in all large cities report a dramatic increase in victims of cocaine dependence who are dead on arrival. Continued high use frequently produces a paranoid psychoticlike disorder. The drug is usually snorted—inhaled through the nose—but it is also injected intravenously or smoked, or "freebased." There are five patterns of use: (1) experimental use, (2) recreational use, (3) task-specific use, (4) regular use, and (5) severe addiction.

Addiction almost inevitably follows frequent recreational use. Any person who even experiments with cocaine puts himself at high risk to be captured by this "gift of the Sun God," or "third scourge of mankind" (after alcohol and morphine–heroin), as it has been called.

Addiction to any drug, including alcohol, has been defined as compulsion, loss of control, and continued use in spite of adverse consequences. Treatment requires abstinence from cocaine. Withdrawal symptoms of depression, anxiety, and severe lethargy usually do not require any medication and persist for only a few days. Long-term recovery, starting with inpatient structured rehabilitation, addresses those emotions and thoughts that predate a cocaine relapse.

In the group process, discussion topics usually include

cocaine dreams, drug hunger, addictive thinking, and high-risk situations. Unless these issues are dealt with, reestablishment of the addiction is likely. Any program of chemical dependency recovery must have at its core the basic Twelve Steps of A.A., which have been adopted for a lifelong commitment for cocaine addicts by Cocaine Anonymous.

QUESTION: What is this new drug called "rope" by some of its young users?

ANSWER: Rope is one of the many street names for a powerful drug used in the induction of anesthesia for minor or major surgical procedures. Like Valium and other tranquilizers, rope is a benzodiazepine, whose clinical name is flunitrazepam. Its effect on the human body is rapid and lasts from a half hour to eight hours, depending on the dose. Basically, rope is a sedative that produces a sense of dreamy, somnolent euphoria, and has, like all benzodiazepines, the potential to kill. Rope can be taken orally or by injection and is not approved at this time in the United States, but is used as a pre-induction medication for anesthesia in Europe and South America. Newspaper reports from the *Tulsa World* staff writers (Braun and Netherton) describe an almost epidemic increase in the abuse of this drug in the Tulsa, Oklahoma, school districts. Young people who take the drug experience a rapid sedating effect, from drowsiness to unconsciousness. Rope is also called "roofies" and "forget-me-nots." The Oklahoma state legislature has enacted a law that makes this substance a schedule I controlled drug, in the class with heroin, LSD, PCP, and other such chemicals not legally available in this country.

OTHER SUBSTANCES

QUESTION: What about caffeine—is it an addicting drug?

ANSWER: For some, yes. Caffeine is currently the most widely used psychoactive drug in the world. With low doses, a cup of coffee or two, people usually feel mild positive effects, such as increased feelings of well-being, energy, and alertness, whereas higher doses cause nervousness and anxiety. But be aware that there are also withdrawal symptoms when one abruptly stops caffeine consumption that include headaches, lethargy, and mild depression. These withdrawal symptoms disappear after a day or two of abstinence from caffeine.

While most immediately think of coffee as the main caffeine source, in a study from the Johns Hopkins University School of Medicine, soft drinks served as the main source of caffeine for almost half of the caffeine-dependent subjects.

With caffeine, moderation is the key.

QUESTION: Is nicotine a drug? Is it addicting? If it's a drug, why isn't it regulated by the FDA?

ANSWER: The authorities in Washington are considering these questions right now. But we know for certain that nicotine has a definite effect on the brain. It's clear that the more you use nicotine, the more you want it, and hence the more dependent you become. According to the *British Journal of Addiction*, "The adolescent who smokes from four to five cigarettes a day is at very substantial risk of embarking upon several decades of smoking." There are exceedingly few social or recreational smokers, which seems to further point to the addictive qualities of nicotine.

QUESTION: Can steroid use be dangerous?

ANSWER: Yes, it has caused sudden deaths (Kennedy, M., and Lawrence, C., *Medical Journal of Australia* 346–347, 1993). The cause of death is probably a heart rhythm disorder associated with widespread patches of scar tissue in the heart muscle. Although it's not clear why, the fibrotic changes in the muscle tissue, which cause the scarring, interrupt the pathway, hence disturbing the rhythm of the heart. Long-term use of steroids also leads to tumors in the liver, reduction in male hormone production, and changes in behavior, making the user irritable and aggressive.

QUESTION: Besides building muscle, what effect do steroids have?

ANSWER: Steroids are synthetic analogs of the male hormone testosterone. These substances have gained a reputation in the athletic underground for producing increased muscle mass. There are unwelcome and distressing mental side effects that come about with massive doses of this substance that some athletes usually take. Steroids in the amount necessary to effect great muscle mass have caused takers to show uncommon aggression, occasional violence, irritability, and in some, psychotic symptoms of paranoid or grandiose illusions. Increased feelings of confidence, euphoria, grandiosity, and power are part of the reinforcement process associated with addiction to steroids.

Physical effects include a shutdown of natural testosterone production with testicle atrophy, and tumors of the liver. These physical complications sometimes occur after long-term, high-dose use and are frequently reversible when use is stopped. Depression is a common withdrawal symptom following abrupt cessation of steroid use.

Question: I understand that there is a new hormone that young athletes are taking to enhance their performance. Could you comment?

Answer: The hormone you are referring to is human growth hormone (HGH), which is taken to increase muscle growth. So far, there is not a lot of information about how widespread the use of HGH may be, but if it follows the pattern of steroid abuse (surveys published in *Bottom Line* have shown that 5 to 7 percent of male high school students have used anabolic steroids), there may be reason for concern. The adverse consequences of this abuse are yet to be determined, but it is highly probable that there will be some negative effects on abusers of HGH, who don't meet the rather rare clinical indication for its prescribed and monitored use.

CROSS ADDICTIONS AND DUAL DISORDERS

PERSONS WITH ADDICTIVE disease are no more prone to other mental illnesses than the general population. Cross addiction implies that if a person is a victim dependent on one psychoactive substance he is at high risk to develop dependence on any other addicting psychoactive substance. However, when someone suffers from an entirely unrelated anxiety disorder or depression in addition to an addictive disease such as alcoholism or drug abuse, they possess what is called a dual disorder. It is wise, then, to consider the complexities involved with any addictive disease and to keep in mind the interplay of any two diagnoses.

Question: Does a dual diagnosis mean that a person has a certain kind of alcoholism?

Answer: Someone who has a dual diagnosis suffers from both a substance use disorder (alcoholism or drug addiction) and a major mental disorder (psychosis, depression, personality disorder, severe anxiety disorder). People with dual diagnoses need to be treated for both conditions.

Question: I have been diagnosed as having bipolar disease and have been prescribed lithium for several years. During the last year, I began to drink heavily, so I entered a treatment center where I completed four weeks of treatment. I feel so good now that I am not drinking, I am thinking of quitting the lithium. What do you think?

Answer: Don't stop taking the lithium! Bipolar disease, also known as manic-depressive illness, and addictive disease are two different kinds of sicknesses, each with its own treatment. Continue with the lithium and periodic lithium blood level tests. Also follow the prescribed aftercare counseling and A.A. for your alcoholism. Always consult with your psychiatrist about the further need for lithium before you stop taking it.

QUESTION: My son is a recovering heroin addict and thinks he can have a beer or two now and then. He feels it will help him assuage his cravings. He has never had any problems with alcohol, but I would welcome your opinion. I've also noticed that since his abstinence his desire for sweets has increased appreciably. Any harm there?

ANSWER: A beer or two now and then is risky for a person recovering from heroin addiction, and here's why. Heroin addiction and alcoholism are different forms of the same disorder, called addictive disease. People with this disease share a common powerful potential to become addicted to any psychoactive drug of the euphoriant class (alcohol, cocaine, opioids, sedative–hypnotics, cannabis, etc.), and recovering from one of these substances does not mean that the person is then immune to the development of an equally binding addiction to another drug, even if he or she has never used the drug before. In other words, to this vulnerable victim of addictive disease, all drugs that produce a "high" (euphoria) are cross-addicting. It is not uncommon for the person who tries other drugs, usually alcohol, to find that it leads, in a short time, back to that original drug of choice—in your son's case, heroin—from which he had been successfully abstinent for a while.

About the sugars and sweets—tell him to stick to them. Although there is no scientific evidence that fully explains the tendency, heroin addicts seem to crave sugar, which is not harmful when taken in moderation.

QUESTION: Is there a link between domestic violence and drinking?

ANSWER: In about half of the cases of domestic violence, alcohol is involved. But, according to professionals who work in this field, alcohol cannot be targeted as a direct cause of domestic violence. However, in any home where alcohol abuse exists, there tends to be violence, whether it be physical, verbal, or emotional.

QUESTION: I have a depression for which I have been prescribed a monoamine oxidase inhibitor (MAOI). Is drinking alcohol not recommended? I do not have an alcohol problem.

ANSWER: It is absolutely not recommended. In fact, your physician has no doubt told you that many other prescription and over-the-counter drugs will react adversely with your MAOI antidepressant. Also, you should avoid foods such as aging cheese and those with a high tyramine content, including Chianti wine, sherry, beer (including nonalcoholic beer), and pickled foods. Ask your doctor for a list of all the foods you should avoid. Hypertensive crises, also known as critical blood pressure elevation, have sometimes occurred during MAOI therapy after ingestion of foods with a high tyramine content. Having or not having an alcohol problem has nothing to do with this. Be safe; drink absolutely no alcohol.

QUESTION: How do some people get hooked on cocaine while others become addicted to other drugs, including alcohol?

ANSWER: People addicted to any one of these drugs are potentially addicted to all; addicting drugs are all cross-addicting. People tend to seek out a drug for its effect and/or its availability. This is not a random or accidental choice, but a profound identification of the desired way in which the drug successfully alters one's consciousness. In other words, the drug of dependence meets a special and powerful psychological need. Those who have addictive disease will usually become dependent on a drug if they use it enough; those who do not have addictive disease will emerge from experimentation and recreational use as occasional users, or will stop use entirely. Anyone with addictive disease brings a susceptibility to addiction to their first use of any addicting substance, including alcohol, the only legally available nonprescription psychoactive drug.

Drugs of dependence have a spectrum of pharmacological effects ranging from extreme and euphoric exhilaration (cocaine); inhibition suppression and relaxation with reduction of anxieties (alcohol, tranquilizers, sedatives); euphoria, relaxation, vivid imagery, and heightened sexual arousal (marijuana); and a profound and dreamy euphoria, detachment, reduction of aggressive and sexual drives, drowsiness, and a deep feeling of emotional well-being (opioids, heroin, morphine). Each of these basic chemicals has as its target organ the brain, and each has different receptors in the brain. All of these drugs engage the reward network of the brain, or the operative neurological machinery of drug addiction.

QUESTION: I am a recovering alcoholic and have been dry for twenty-two years. My wife died five weeks ago and my physician, who does not know my alcoholism history, prescribed a tranquilizer called diazepam for my insomnia and my depression. Am I safe taking these?

ANSWER: No, you are not safe taking diazepam, or other drugs like it. You should tell your doctor that you are a recovering alcoholic and he will know that, even though you have been abstinent for twenty-two years, you are at high risk for relapse to active addiction if you start taking a sedative drug. All psychoactive drugs are cross-addicting in the person with addictive disease. The sedative effects of the tranquilizer could reactivate your long-arrested alcoholism. Alcohol is also a psychoactive drug and a sedative: your brain would immediately recognize the tranquilizer as an old friend. You need to stop by your doctor's office again and provide him or her with all of the information you have given me. Your doctor should then be able to help you in the safest and most effective way possible.

QUESTION: How many people who are alcoholic have a mental disorder?

ANSWER: Alcoholism is a mental or behavioral disorder, so I would say all of them. A comprehensive study of the United States population at large (Regiar, D.L., et al. The De Facto U.S. Mental and Addictive Disorders Service System. *Archives of General Psychiatry*, Feb. 1993) showed that of the total sample, 13.5 percent received an alcohol-related diagnosis, and of this group 22.3 percent had an additional psychiatric diagnosis. An anxiety disorder is the most frequent psychiatric condition to accompany alcoholism. Fortunately, the vast majority of those people suffering from a dual disorder respond successfully to the psychotherapeutic and behavioral modification measures used in standard alcoholism treatment centers. Occasionally, a more severe anxiety, or phobic condition, requires a nonaddicting medication in addition to alcoholism therapy.

QUESTION: What is an antisocial personality? My son has been in a couple of treatment centers for alcohol and drugs and now is back in jail after resisting arrest while drunk. He was told that he has a drinking problem, along with an antisocial personality disorder.

ANSWER: Antisocial personality disorder is one of the most difficult conditions to treat and, although quite uncommon, the odds of having alcoholism with it are very high. Because of the great complexity of this particular disorder, I do not want to go into this any further here, but I would strongly urge you to get into a family treatment program and also call Al-Anon for your own support and mental health. For further information concerning your son's diagnosis of antisocial personality disorder, I recommend you consult with a psychiatrist.

QUESTION: I have been dry four years and I don't belong to any sobriety organization. I've used my own willpower to stop drinking. Two and one half months ago, I had some business reversals and I had great difficulty sleeping. My doctor prescribed a mild nerve pill, which helps me to sleep all right, but I have the same feeling I had after a drink or two. The name of the pill is diazepam.

ANSWER: My guess is the reason you have written is that you feel you're on dangerous ground. Let me reinforce your concerns: You are at risk of either becoming hooked on these pills (patented name, Valium) or going back to that other more addicting drug—alcohol. When you say that you've been dry for four years, I presume that prior to that you were drinking addictively. All addictions have in common (1) compulsion, (2) loss of control, and (3) continued use in spite of adverse consequences. People with addictive diseases are potentially addicted to all psychoactive drugs, and the tranquilizer you are taking qualifies as one of these. Also, I suggest that having quit this drug as of now, you give A.A. a try.

If you had sought the help of A.A. earlier, you would have known the danger for an alcoholic of taking a tranquilizer. Education about your addictive disease is one of the many benefits A.A. provides.

QUESTION: I am a 42-year-old woman and an alcoholic. In addition, I take lithium as directed and am monitored by my psychiatrist for manic-depressive illness. My question is—would I be accepted for treatment in an alcohol treatment center?

ANSWER: Yes. You would be welcome and, since it is not uncommon for those suffering from manic-depressive illness to also suffer from alcohol abuse, good treatment centers have the experience and expertise to help you with your specific situation. The treatment center would be in contact with your psychiatrist to keep him or her informed about your treatment and to give recommendations for your aftercare follow-up, which would be coordinated with the requirements of your psychiatric care. During your stay in the treatment center, you would continue taking lithium and therapeutic levels would be maintained by regular monitoring.

QUESTION: I am a schizophrenic and have been getting along okay for many years as long as I take my Haldol. I started drinking heavily two years ago and was referred to A.A., which has helped me to stop drinking. But I am concerned because someone in A.A. questioned whether I can still take Haldol and be considered clean and sober. Would it be wise to stop my medication?

ANSWER: Do not stop taking the Haldol prescribed. You have two disorders: schizophrenia and alcoholism. The Haldol controls the symptoms of your schizophrenia, and if you stopped taking the drug, then your symptoms would only recur. Do not change your medication schedule without the consent of your psychiatrist. Some well-meaning friends in A.A. probably do not understand the nature of your illness, nor do they know that Haldol is not an addicting drug. You have what we call a dual disorder, and as long as you need and take your medication, you can participate fully and with great fulfillment in the Twelve Steps of A.A.

TREATMENT

TREATMENT OF ADDICTIVE disease follows a logical pattern of attending, first, to urgent physical consequences of alcohol and/or drug use. This can take the form of detoxification or the immediate treatment of some life-threatening organic disorder like liver failure. Next comes the major form of care, which focuses on the core of the illness. Since addictive disease is primarily a behavioral disorder, the treatment consists of psychotherapy, which identifies and deals with irrational feelings and distorted thinking associated with and aggravated by chronic alcohol or drug abuse. At the heart of the disease, however, is the necessity for deep reckoning with personal and family history, and treatment centers are commonly the site where recovery from alcohol and drug addiction is started and directed. However, permanent recovery is most often accomplished through continued involvement in self-help groups, such as Alcoholics Anonymous.

TREATMENT: GETTING HELP

QUESTION: How long does alcohol withdrawal last? I ended my last binge twenty-seven days ago and I'm still shaky and cannot sleep. I started going to A.A. and have been going daily since that last drink. When do I start feeling better?

ANSWER: Soon; hang in there. It really *does* get better. Because you were a heavy drinker, you are still experiencing what is called protracted withdrawal syndrome. Signs and symptoms of this state include physiological and psychological variations, such as unstable blood pressure, respiratory irregularity, irritability, anxiety, insomnia, and depressed mood. In addition to these symptoms, you may have surges of cravings for a drink. These are the times to call one of your new friends in A.A. who can tell you how he or she got through this challenging period. You are nearing the end of this distressing time of your recovery and, after it passes, you'll get even more out of what you hear at your daily A.A. meetings. Eat a balanced diet, take vitamins, particularly the vitamin B complex, do some simple exercise, and check with your physician to be sure that you haven't incurred some physical condition that needs attention. Don't give up!

QUESTION: What do you think about trying to quit smoking while I'm undergoing treatment for alcoholism?

ANSWER: I think it's a good idea. It used to be thought that dealing with one addiction at a time is enough, but a study at the Mayo Clinic (Hunt, R.D., Eberman, K.M., et al. Nicotine Dependent Treatment During Inpatient Treatment for Other Addiction. *Alcoholism, Clinical and Experimental Research* 1994; 18) showed that the process of treatment for one addiction, such as alcohol, enhances the effectiveness of dealing with the other, in your case, nicotine. The number of deaths due to alcoholism, 100,000+, and tobacco, 450,000+, annually, makes the idea of dealing with alcohol and nicotine together not only a good idea, but a life-extending one.

QUESTION: After my last two binges, I began to see things and hear threatening voices that I knew weren't there. The visions left after about twelve hours, but the voices still come back every now and then. Was this the D.T.'s? Is this going to happen every time I drink?

ANSWER: No, this was not the D.T.'s (delirium tremens), and yes, it probably will happen every time after you come off a binge. This problem—called alcoholic hallucinosis—occurs in persons with a long drinking history; it is uncommon and occurs in the presence of an otherwise perfectly clear sensorium. Why the brain responds in this way to this stage of alcohol withdrawal is not completely understood.

Fortunately, this reaction is not accompanied by the severe physical and mental complications of delirium tremens. However, the characteristic intermittent hearing of voices can last for months. All of this implies that there is some brain damage, possibly reversible if you stay sober.

QUESTION: What is the eventual outlook for the severe alcoholic who won't or can't quit?

ANSWER: There is a typical profile of that end-stage career. The alcoholic begins to narrow his or her drinking repertoire, with little day-to-day variability in the beverage choice, scheduling drinking to maintain a high blood alcohol level. Then he or she gives obtaining alcohol the highest priority while experiencing an increasingly high tolerance for alcohol since the alcoholic can now function at a blood alcohol level that would normally incapacitate a person. Frequently a person at this stage also experiences severe withdrawal symptoms, including tremors, hallucinations, seizures, and delirium tremens. So, he or she drinks primarily to ward off withdrawal symptoms. A person at this stage has an awareness of loss of control over alcohol intake, accompanied by intense craving for alcohol with even a slightly reduced intake. Finally, if such a person is able to become alcohol-free for weeks, months, or even years, should drinking start again, it will revert to the old stereotype pattern in just days. Liver and brain damage have already occurred at this stage, but even now, treatment can help.

QUESTION: Are a few drinks taken at five- or six-hour intervals a good way to detox from months of heavy drinking—about a quart of whiskey a day?

ANSWER: No, there is a better way. Although this method was used in centuries past, there were many poor souls who braved the experience of delirium tremens; some lived and some died. Modern care of acute alcohol withdrawal syndrome offers safety and a great deal less pain than taking some of the "hair of the dog that bit you." The treatment of severe alcohol withdrawal syndrome is, however, a medical emergency and requires expert care provided in treatment centers. Contact a professional treatment center. Your local A.A. chapter will have a list of local ones.

QUESTION: How does Antabuse work? If, as I was told, it makes a person sick if he drinks, why would any other treatment be necessary?

ANSWER: Antabuse (disulfiram) works by blocking the removal of a toxic substance (acetaldehyde) that occurs in the liver when alcohol is broken down, or metabolized. A special enzyme, acetaldehyde dehydrogenase, which rids the liver and bloodstream of this substance, is the target of Antabuse. Flushing, a tight feeling in the chest, headache, and more or less severe discomfort are experienced by the person who takes a drink after taking Antabuse. The effect of a dose of Antabuse usually lasts from twenty-four to forty-eight hours. This very unpleasant consequence of drinking alcohol while taking Antabuse does not address at all the mental and emotional symptoms at the root of alcoholism. Antabuse is occasionally helpful in getting a person through a severe period of craving experienced early in recovery, but these benefits have generally not been effective in maintaining long-term sobriety.

QUESTION: What is this new drug naltrexone? Is it the cure for alcoholism?

ANSWER: First off, naltrexone is not a new drug. It has been used for a number of years to deter the use of opioids (heroin, morphine, and the like) by blocking the opium receptor sites in the brain that are involved with the euphoric or high response to drugs. Naltrexone was tried on a number of alcoholics (groups of 70 and 104) in one study (Volpicelli, J.R., Alterman, A.L., et al. Naltrexone in the Treatment of Alcohol Dependence. *Archives of General Psychiatry* 49: 876–880, 1992), and it was reported that the rate of relapse decreased by about half from the control group in a three-month period. It was also reported that some people experienced a reduced craving; others claimed that it reduced the high that alcohol provided. The effect of the drug in alcoholics appears to have an action similar to the way it works with opioid addicts. However, naltrexone is not a cure for alcoholism, nor is it in any way a treatment for alcoholism. The treatment of alcoholism involves a complete psychological, spiritual, and emotional shift, whereby victims of the disease are released at the core of their being from the compulsion to drink, as the result of a conscious and unconscious adoption of a set of principles and values that set them free from the bondage of the disease. Naltrexone can do none of these things, nor was it ever designed or expected to. However, though the studies involve too small a sample to assess the long-term value of the drug, naltrexone, like disulfiram, may play a role in helping a person reduce or even stop drinking enough to start treatment. It may be very effective in preventing relapse.

QUESTION: When I had my last drink on July 21, 1962, I started in A.A. and they were always encouraging me to drink orange juice with some honey while coming off the booze, or any time anxiety started up. This seemed to help a lot. Why is this?

141

Answer: Weaning one's self off nine to twelve cans of beer is being done by countless beer drinkers across the country with little more than a sense of discomfort, irritability, tremulousness, some sweating, and a greater or lesser craving for that can of beer that they know will "settle things down." Rarely does a person have severe withdrawal symptoms from that amount of regular consumption unless there exists a serious state of malnutrition. Persons who abruptly stop drinking nine to twelve daily beers because of the onset of a major illness, such as pneumonia, or who are victims of a serious injury are prone to severe withdrawal symptoms or delirium tremens, which can be life threatening. But in an otherwise healthy person, efforts to "get off the stuff" are part of the history of most persons who finally make it to A.A. They learn that it's not the quitting that counts, it's the keeping from starting up again.

Now about the orange juice and honey: whatever works (and is safe, and even tastes good) is okay. Science has not made any public pronouncements on this mixture, but we know from experience that science often lags behind what people have known and used for centuries.

Question: Since treatment is so available all over the country now, why are an increasing number of people suffering from substance abuse?

ANSWER: More people with substance abuse disorder are being identified; however, according to the National Association of Addiction Treatment Providers (NAATP), currently only 15 percent of substance abusers who need treatment get it. Less than one third of 1 percent of insured workers receive inpatient treatment for alcohol and drug dependency. Federally funded programs are overloaded. Most private programs are operating well below capacity; more than 300 such programs have closed their doors in the past three years because of lack of patients.

The costs associated with untreated substance abuse are high: an estimated 10 to 23 percent of workers use illegal drugs; an estimated 6 to 16 percent of workers are alcoholic. As a result, these groups combined miss 500 million workdays per year, costing $20 billion annually. Lost productivity due to alcoholism and drug dependence cost $40 billion in 1988, with more than $33 billion attributed to alcohol use. Up to half of all hospitalized patients suffer from alcohol-related illness or accidents.

The problem, NAATP says, is that currently public policy casts addiction as a crime, not an illness. Consequently, managed care feels free to single out substance abuse treatment as an easy target for benefit reductions, or elimination, in the private sector. At the same time, inadequate appropriations and Medicaid restrictions hamper the effectiveness and restrict the capacity of public programs. The basic fact is that treatment works, but that it is not being implemented to the extent that it should. It is cost effective, it saves lives and prevents wasteful use of health care resources. There is a dire need for a federal policy that encourages and implements greater access to substance abuse treatment.

QUESTION: Why can some people make it sober and others can't even though they try? My son died two years ago while drinking and driving his speedboat alone. He drowned. I'm just now able to talk about it. He had been through two treatment programs and went to A.A. for a while.

ANSWER: I offer my deepest condolences to you. He tried, and had he persisted, which he hopefully would have, he probably would have made it, had it not been for that tragic boating accident. People who don't quit trying for permanent sobriety, in spite of many relapses, almost invariably make it. However, not infrequently, a tragic event interrupts a halting but persistent effort. Drowning is the number four cause of accidental death in the United States and is related to alcohol use about half or more of the time.

I hope you have had the opportunity to get some help with your grief.

QUESTION: Can you tell me what the chances are for a person who goes through a treatment program of getting sober and staying sober?

ANSWER: What you are really asking is what the recovery rates are for a person who completes a treatment program. Whether a person goes through a residential inpatient program or an outpatient program depends on the severity of the addiction. A study of 65,000 patients followed after completing treatment (CATOR independent treatment outcome evaluation service, St. Paul, MN, 1994) showed that about 60 percent maintain total and continuing abstinence the first year. The average number breaks down like this: Of those patients who attend self-help support groups (A.A.) at least weekly for one year, 73 percent will be sober; of those who attend only occasionally, 53 percent will be sober; and of those who never went or who quit going, 44 percent will have maintained sobriety. Rates of abstinence for those who are involved with once- or twice-weekly continuing professional care show that at 12 months, 85 percent of those who followed through will have maintained sobriety; for those who drop out from 6 to 11 months, 70 percent will have been abstinent; for those who stick it out only for 1 to 5 months, 55 percent will have continuous sobriety. And those who don't follow the recommended continuing care at all will show a 56 percent rate of abstinence. Persons who attend self-support groups, like A.A., and also are faithful to regular continuing care with a professional have the highest recovery rate—in excess of 85 percent.

It is expected that those who attend A.A. will continue involvement on a permanent basis. Patients will encounter the most risks for relapse in the first year following treatment. These risks take the form of a variety of emotional, interpersonal, and possibly financial or legal problems, which can be best dealt with by continuing regular self-help support group attendance and professional services. In summary, people who complete treatment but who don't follow through with either self-help support group attendance or regular continuing professional contacts have a less than 50 percent chance of staying sober; those who follow through with both have a greater than 80 percent probability of permanent sobriety.

QUESTION: What kind of training do physicians get in medical school about alcoholism and drug addiction?

ANSWER: It is considerably more and much better now than when I went through medical school. At that time, in the 1930s and 1940s, alcoholism meant "skid row," "cirrhosis of the liver," "patients to avoid," "they mess up your waiting room," "they never pay," etc.

Since 1955, when alcoholism was defined as a disease by the American Medical Association, medical schools' curricula started to include not only the physiological changes in the alcoholic, but also the psychological and social dimensions of the disease.

One of the most sophisticated and effective programs for medical students was established nine years ago at the Betty Ford Center in its Medical Student Summer School for Alcoholism. Here the medical student, having learned about the physical and psychological aspects of the illness in medical school, experiences one week in the treatment process as a patient. The student learns that there is an effective treatment for alcoholism and lo, these people suffering from alcoholism are just like everybody else, including him or her. Moving beyond the judgmental mode to the empathetic one when thinking of those with addictive disease is important for all of us as a society. We have come a long way and hopefully we will continue to consider this disease as just that—a disease.

QUESTION: Is it true that you have to wait for a person to "hit bottom" before you can do anything about it? I know you have to wait until a person who is killing himself with liquor wants to quit. Isn't there anything that can be done before he wrecks his life, as well as those of his three kids and mine?

ANSWER: Yes, there is something that can be done, and *should* be done. First, let me correct some very wrong ideas you have about hitting bottom, and his having to want to quit. These are old ideas that have been proven false by the experience of thousands of alcoholics (just like your husband, as you describe in your letter) who have been "motivated" to get help, usually in a treatment center or A.A. This motivation is called an intervention, and it can be as informal as persuading him to get help, to which, at this stage, he may not respond. If this is the case, you may apply some sanctions, such as taking the kids and leaving unless he agrees to get help.

A more formal kind of intervention can be done using a professional interventionist who will spend some time teaching the family and other concerned persons—not in the presence of the alcoholic—just how this process works. After this preparation and rehearsal, the alcoholic is included in the gathering, almost always as a surprise to him, lest he refuse to come. Emotions, expressions of love, recounting by the children of very frightening times, threat of job loss by the employer, who you might want to include as part of the process, disclosure by you of a plan to leave, will take place at this meeting. The goal of the intervention is to get the alcoholic into treatment, and this way of doing it works about 80 percent of the time.

In the past two decades, interventions have been shown to be a most effective tool in the eventual recovery of alcoholics and other drug users. It has also become clear that the attitude of resistance by the alcoholic changes once he gets into treatment. As insight develops with therapy, the person becomes an active participant in his treatment. Finally, when it becomes clear that a family member, employee, or friend is suffering from alcoholism, strategies starting with suggestions and progressing all the way to formal intervention, if necessary, should be put into motion.

QUESTION: Do prayers help in trying to get an alcoholic to stop drinking?

ANSWER: Sometimes, it seems, they're the only things that do. Hope, and the internal spiritual strengths that respond to prayer, can sustain the person who has to stand by and watch an alcoholic tragedy unfold. However, people have told me many times that after they have prayed, help has shown up in the most unexpected place and time.

Incidentally, I would like you to call the treatment center in your community and make arrangements to get into their family treatment program now. Because of the dire financial straits of your being unemployed while your wife is at home drunk with three young children, as you mention in your letter, ask for the generous financial assistance program this particular treatment center has for those who can't afford the cost of treatment. But, also, do keep praying.

QUESTION: Does taking a cold shower or drinking a couple of cups of strong coffee sober a person up faster? It doesn't seem to work when I try to sober up my friends.

ANSWER: It doesn't work for anybody else either. The body rids itself of alcohol on a fixed schedule. The liver metabolizes 1 ounce of 100-proof whiskey (or one 12-ounce can of beer, or one 5-ounce glass of wine) per hour. This comes out to ½ ounce of absolute alcohol per hour, and with rare exceptions, it occurs no faster or no slower no matter what is done. So, if your friends, or even you, were to drink ten drinks in one or two hours, it would take five hours for the blood alcohol to go down to a level just below legal intoxication (.08) and ten hours to reach a blood alcohol level of 0 percent. At this time, there is no drug that can restore sobriety quickly as can be done for narcotic overdose with Narcan. So, while a cold shower may make sobering up a cleaner experience, it has no effect on the rate of lowering the blood alcohol level. Coffee can only add the inevitable jitters one can expect during that regrettable ten hours it takes for the above-mentioned amount of alcohol to leave the body.

ALCOHOLICS ANONYMOUS

QUESTION: What is the success rate of Alcoholics Anonymous? I have never seen it published.

ANSWER: Every few years Alcoholics Anonymous does a survey of its members. In 1992, a random survey of 6,500 A.A. members in both the United States and Canada revealed that 35 percent were sober for more than five years; 34 percent were sober from between one and five years; and 31 percent were sober for less than one year. The average time sobriety of members is more than five years. According to A.A. World Services, the survey is designed to provide information to the professional community and the general public as part of its purpose to carry the message of recovery to those who still suffer from alcoholism. For more information about Alcoholics Anonymous, write to A.A. World Services, Grand Central Station, Box 459, New York, NY 10163.

QUESTION: I've been through a treatment center for alcoholism. At the time, the staff thought I should stay in treatment there for five weeks, which I did. Anyway I'm out now, and I think I've learned almost everything there is to know about staying dry. I was told by my counselor that I should attend A.A. I went a couple of times, but I knew more about alcoholism than most of the people there, even though a lot of them have been sober a long time. What more can I learn?

ANSWER: How to stay sober for a long time. A piece of knowledge you may have missed is that you must go to any length to achieve permanent sobriety, and that going to A.A. meetings is one of the most essential lengths. Technical information about the disease has little or nothing to do with avoiding that next drink. If you don't understand this essential premise, you have much to learn. Please go to ninety meetings in ninety days and then check your knowledge bank. Take it on faith from me that those long-time-sober people in the meetings probably know a few things that you don't.

QUESTION: Can a person be expelled from A.A. if he keeps having slips?

ANSWER: No! As a matter of fact, until a decade or so ago, alcoholism was defined in the medical literature as a disorder characterized by relapses. The behavior of the "slipper" merely confirms the thoughts of most medical people who are not familiar with the vast number of alcoholics who have recovered. For many alcoholics, all of their relapses occurred before they got into Alcoholics Anonymous; for others, who just can't seem to "make it," relapses continue to plague their lives. A relapse can be an impressive, though painful and possibly fatal, educational experience. Repeated slips happen because there is some fundamental flaw in an effort to quit drinking and "stay on the program."

Whether you have asked this question for yourself or for a friend or relative, I want you to know that there are specific treatment techniques designed to deal with chronic relapse. This is one of the identifiable indications for getting professional help, ideally in an inpatient or intensive outpatient program. Whether the slip is a short-term, low-consequence relapse or a major alcoholic catastrophe, success is always possible and probable if the person in question is persistent in his or her wish for sobriety and continues to attend A.A.

QUESTION: I go to A.A. meetings every week or so, but I am turned off by the religious tone of the discussions.

I relate to the drinking stories of the other members and they seem to have helped me stay sober so far, but I don't understand what the God part has to do with it.

ANSWER: A quote from that great psychiatrist Carl Jung, who was also a close friend of Bill Wilson, the founder of A.A., expresses the answer to this good question better than I can: "Among all my patients in the second half of life—that is to say over 35—there has not been one whose problem in the last resort was not that of finding a religious outlook on life. It is safe to say that every one of them fell ill because he had lost what the living religions of every age have given to their followers, and none of them is really healed who did not regain his religious outlook. This, of course, has nothing to do with a particular creed or membership in a church" (Carl Jung, *Collected Works,* Vol. 11, p. 334). I think this quote really addresses the role of spirituality in recovery.

QUESTION: Is it necessary to go to A.A. meetings for life? How long does treatment for alcoholism take?

ANSWER: Yes. Treatment takes as long as a person has alcoholism, which is, a lifetime. As with diabetes, heart disease, rheumatoid arthritis, and other similar chronic illnesses, the treatment is ongoing. The goal of treatment in all these conditions, including alcoholism, is to establish a steady state of optimal health and functioning. This means that the destructive symptoms of the disease are arrested, but in some diseases like alcoholism, diabetes, and others, there is not a cure.

In alcoholism, a cure would imply a person could drink alcohol like nonalcoholic persons without loss of control and with an eventual return to continued drinking without any adverse consequences. Experience has taught us there is no return to controlled drinking. But, abstinence does not come automatically and permanently after an initial treatment experience. Recovery from alcoholism requires an ongoing consciousness of the nature of the illness and the risks of relapse. In fact, for the rest of the recovering alcoholic's life, he or she must exercise principles that are the essentials of relapse prevention.

With the majority of recovering alcoholics, there is a lifelong, continued involvement in the program of Alcoholics Anonymous with its foundation of spirituality, mental health, and powerful social support.

QUESTION: I am in the ninth year of my sobriety, and for the last three years have attended A.A. perhaps once a year, at most. During the first seven years, I had a wonderful analysis and in the final year my therapist's goal was to wean me away from A.A. He's familiar with and supportive of the program, but claims that my progress, growth, and insight were so strong that A.A. and its "peer counseling" were restrictive to my growth. I am not better than anyone else, and I am grateful to A.A. for starting me on the road to recovery. I have no desire to drink, and if I meet a newcomer to AA socially I help them. But I feel that A.A. is no longer in my best interest after seven or so years. Your feedback please!

ANSWER: Your letter tells me that you have been an active member of A.A. for about seven years, and it also says that you have accepted the premise that you are an alcoholic, and that the principles of the program started you on the road to recovery. Since the steps of the A.A. program form the foundation for a life of mental and emotional health, I can't reconcile the idea that continued participation in the program could constitute a restriction to your personal growth.

You also mention A.A. and its "peer counseling" as being something that you have moved beyond as part of your therapy. My feedback is that peer counseling is not a part of A.A., but that individual sharing of experiences, strengths, and hopes is. In fact, the interaction in the A.A. group setting is a powerful form of therapy which, for years, has met the mental and spiritual needs of the recovering participants.

People of every level of education find the principles of A.A. sufficient to maintain sobriety. Occasionally, persons in A.A. get stuck in their progress toward comfortable sobriety and find that a few sessions with a mental health professional are very helpful. But the primary purpose of any professional counseling for the

A.A. member is to help him or her better use the program, rather than disengage from it.

Finally, I understand your question, and appreciate it, but I believe the best course includes continued involvement in A.A. (if you are truly alcoholic), and whatever other helpful therapy you wish.

QUESTION: What is this business of having an A.A. birthday?

ANSWER: It is a serious business indeed. It marks a successful passage from one year to another in sobriety. The tradition of this kind of celebration is more prevalent in California than in some other parts of the country, but the custom is spreading. It has a very powerful meaning to the celebrants and the witnesses of the event: THE PROGRAM WORKS. Birthdays of this kind may seem to the nonalcoholic person a trivial and empty event, but to the recovering alcoholic the celebration has joyously important meaning, for it is on the A.A. birthday that the celebrant experiences the first effects of freedom from the imprisonment of her or his addiction. An important part of this celebration is that the "birthday person" tells the story of what it was like in the grip of alcoholism, and how on that great day A.A. started the gradual return to sanity and health, and what it is like now, be it one, ten, thirty, or fifty years of sobriety later. The shaky newcomer sees the real message of this celebration as saying, "This program works, and if he or she can do it, I can do it."

QUESTION: How can I start an A.A. group? I live in an isolated ranch area, and the nearest town (population 3,500) is 15 miles away. I got sober four years ago and moved here to work a month ago. I was told there was no A.A. in the town.

ANSWER: Here's what you do—it is what Bill Wilson, founder of A.A., did, in June of 1935, in Akron, Ohio. Call the clergyman in whatever church there is in that nearest town. A minister or priest can probably tell you if there is someone in his flock who needs and hopefully wants what you have in your sobriety and help direct your efforts to organize a meting. Who knows, the clergyman may even let you use his church basement for A.A. meetings. This could be the beginning of a wondrous thing in your community. And write to Alcoholics Anonymous, Grand Central Station, Box 459, New York, NY 10163, for more help and literature.

QUESTION: I am a newcomer to A.A. I heard about it and I just started going to meetings. Some in A.A. tell me I need a sponsor. Do you think having a sponsor is absolutely necessary?

ANSWER: Some have made it through recovery without having a sponsor, so I suppose it is not absolutely necessary, but it is an absolutely good idea. This is what A.A. says about it in its official literature: "Essentially, the process of sponsorship is this: an alcoholic who has made some progress in the recovery program shares that experience on a continuous, individual basis with another alcoholic who is attempting to attain or maintain sobriety through A.A."

There are so many benefits of getting a sponsor, not the least of which is always having a person with whom you can share your thoughts and feelings about anything you wish. Developing the most effective relationship with a sponsor takes some time, and not infrequently a person has to try out a couple of sponsors to find the right person. Some of the finest friendships have developed from this idea of sponsorship, and most alcoholics who are recovering find a sponsor an important part of the process.

QUESTION: What are the Twelve Traditions of Alcoholics Anonymous?

ANSWER:

1. Our common welfare should come first; personal recovery depends on A.A. unity.
2. For our group purpose, there is but one ultimate

authority—a loving God as He may express Himself in our group conscience. Our leaders are but trusted servants; they do not govern.

3. The only requirement for A.A. membership is a desire to stop drinking.

4. Each group should be autonomous except in matters affecting other groups or A.A. as a whole.

5. Each group has but one primary purpose—to carry its message to the alcoholic who still suffers.

6. An A.A. group ought never endorse, finance or lend the A.A. name to any related facility or outside enterprise, lest problems of money, property and prestige divert us from our primary purpose.

7. Every A.A. group ought to be fully self-supporting, declining outside contributions.

8. Alcoholics Anonymous should remain forever non-professional, but our service centers may employ special workers.

9. A.A., as such, ought never be organized; but we may create service boards or committees directly responsible to those they serve.

10. Alcoholics Anonymous has no opinion on outside issues; hence the A.A. name ought never to be drawn into public controversy.

11. Our public relations policy is based on attraction rather than promotion; we need always maintain personal anonymity at the level of press, radio and films.

12. Anonymity is the spiritual foundation of all our Traditions, ever reminding us to place principles before personalities.

The Twelve Traditions are reprinted with permission of Alcoholics Anonymous World Services, Inc. Permission to reprint the Twelve Traditions does not mean that A.A. has reviewed or approved the contents of this publication, nor that A.A. agrees with the views expressed herein. A.A. is a program of recovery from alcoholism only—use of the Twelve Traditions in connection with programs and activities which are patterned after A.A., but which address other problems, or in any other non-A.A. context, does not imply otherwise.

QUESTION: What are some of the common reasons people who need alcoholism treatment give for rejecting the idea of going to A.A.?

ANSWER: Here are some and there are probably many, many more:

1. "I am a private person"—"My family never aired their dirty linen in public"—"I've never talked in a group."

2. "Fear of public disclosure"—"This will ruin my career, my reputation"—"What will my family think of me?"—"I don't believe there is anonymity."

3. "I don't need people telling me what to do"— "My life is not out of control"—"I can do it by myself"—"I don't want to lose control of my life."

4. "I can't relate to this group"—"They are worse than me"—"They are not my type"—"They are sick, bad, or crazy."

5. "My work, my schedule, won't permit it"—"I don't have time."

6. "It's a religious cult"—"I don't believe in God"—"I'm not into religion."

7. "I don't understand Alcoholics Anonymous"—"I don't know or believe in what they say, i.e., I'm not sick or diseased."

8. "I don't talk in groups"—"I only discuss things one-on-one."

9. "I'm hopeless"—"If you really knew me, then you would know this wouldn't work"—"I'm too bad an addict"—"I'm really crazy."

10. "If I really have a disease, how can a bunch of amateurs help me?"

11. "My mother would die if she knew I joined A.A."

Oddly enough, most of the people who made these declarations have actually wound up seeking help in Alcoholics Anonymous, simply because the disease caused so much distress in their life they were compelled to reach out for the help that only Alcoholics Anonymous can provide in most instances (Talbott, Doug. Marsh Institute, Atlanta).

QUESTION: I have been in the A.A. program now for about three years and I just don't seem to be able to get the happy, joyous, and free feeling that most of my friends in the program certainly seem to have. I have attended meetings three to five times a week, have a sponsor, and in meetings I always share my thoughts and feelings. But I still feel not quite part of the group, if you know what I mean.

ANSWER: I know exactly what you mean. "There are some people who get stuck at a level of recovery, that is, they are dry but uncomfortable socially, due to anxiety, or because they have never developed a good but realistic image of themselves from which to operate" (Kinney, Jean, M.S.W., and Leaton, Gwen. *Loosening the Grip.* C.V. Mosby Co., St. Louis, Mo. 1978, p. 159).

One of the great things about A.A. is the sense of truly belonging the group provides. But somehow people who carry the extra burden of anxiety don't seem to find it. Many members of A.A. cannot break out of the first stages of the recovery—to get on with life, because of nameless fears, or maybe even just due to a lack of ideas on how to make a more productive or even exciting way of life for themselves. They are stuck without even being aware of their plight, while others in the program are moving happily on. From practice, alcoholics are usually great at handling crises, but once a stable sobriety has been reached, it's time to take some risks for social, career, and certainly give-back kinds of A.A. involvement, along with the regular meetings. There are some in the program who have a real fear of letting go of the life preserver, even when they are safely ashore.

I would suggest that you continue your involvement with A.A. and keep the faith that you will one day have that feeling of inclusion. Finally, I would consider looking into some short-term therapy to deal with self-esteem issues.

QUESTION: How long does a person who has gone through a treatment center have to keep going to A.A.? I feel that I have learned enough in the treatment center to get along without drinking. How about it?

ANSWER: It works this way. You have a chronic disease (alcoholism) characterized by relapse. Experience with people who are recovering has taught us that unless a person constantly renews his commitment to sobriety, his resolve to abstain may totally erode.

There are complex reasons for this. Recovery starts with the penetration of denial, which every person has as a fundamental defense mechanism. In the alcoholic, this takes the form of minimizing the problem or actually believing that drinking alcohol is no problem at all. The mental state that starts the recovery must have, at its depths, the certainty that one is powerless over alcohol and is totally without defense to refrain from the first drink under certain circumstances, and that one will continue drinking in spite of every reason to stop. To accept this powerlessness in the deep recesses of the mind is called surrender. When surrender really happens, denial is fractured into many pieces. To nourish and support this conviction of powerlessness over the ability to stay away from that first drink is the point of continuing involvement in Alcoholics Anonymous. Regular attendance at A.A. meetings and making the Twelve Steps of the A.A. program your way of life keep the surrender intact. Denial, which has been shattered, has a way of reconstituting itself.

QUESTION: I've been hanging around A.A. for years and it hasn't worked. I know all about the steps and all that stuff, I even went to A.A. meetings while I was in prison. I've had the D.T.'s a couple of times. Doctors don't know anything about alcoholism—they just tell me I'm going to die if I don't quit—anyway there are more old drunks than old doctors, ha ha. I've had a couple of drinks just to write this, but I'm just about to give up.

ANSWER: Please don't! In the rest of your letter you mention that you are 62 years old and have lost everything, family, friends, money, a place to live, and, as you say, it's "all because of booze." You've said a couple of things that I think are significant: that you are about to give up, which I hope means that you are ready to surrender to your powerlessness over alcohol and that your life is, and has been for a long time, unmanageable. You have also said that you've lost everything, so you have nothing to lose if you follow my strong recommendation. There are two places in your city called recovery homes. These places provide long-term living and treatment, and because of the environment of sobriety and the extended length of treatment, lives such as yours have been turned around there. There is no person who cannot get better. Call me for the names of these facilities. Incidentally, these recovery homes are, to a great extent, funded by local and state monies, so that your financial state will not be a block to your entry. But *you* have to make the call.

QUESTION: I have been married to an alcoholic for over forty years. I have watched my husband's mother die from alcoholism. That was enough for me but it seems it wasn't for her two sons. My husband goes religiously to A.A. twice a week here in our city. He doesn't enjoy going, but he goes. He said he does need a sponsor and when he asked for one, he was told that their organization wasn't large enough to supply one. What I am asking for is a suggestion. We can't afford for him to go to a private organization for help.

ANSWER: There are some odd features about your question. I must ask first if you have heard of Al-Anon. If you haven't, look them up and join them. You will learn about A.A., and Al-Anon will provide the support and information you will find most helpful.

As for your husband's experience in that A.A. group, it is possible that he misunderstood what he was told about getting a sponsor, but if he has it right, he should join another group. In fact, it doesn't sound like an A.A. group at all, from what you say in the rest of your letter. There are many A.A. groups in your town where any one of the members would be willing to act as a sponsor to your husband. Furthermore, regular attendance at meetings, taking the steps with the help of a sponsor, and perhaps going to A.A. a little more often than twice a week so as to get to know the people in his new group will go a long way toward making both of your lives more fulfilled. Remember—also call Al-Anon.

OTHER TREATMENT ISSUES

QUESTION: How important is addiction treatment in getting over an alcohol problem? Don't most heavy drinkers beat this without ever going to treatment?

ANSWER: Some probably do, but we don't see them, nor is there any documentation in the medical literature to give us the number of victims of alcoholism who recover without some kind of help, including self-help groups or formal therapy programs. Furthermore, just getting dry is only half, or even less, of what defines recovery. Enduring abstinence includes new psychological insights, an improved social life, and the restructuring of values. Treatment consists of helping victims of this disease make these changes.

166

QUESTION: What is the difference between outpatient and inpatient alcohol treatment? Are there any special advantages of one over the other?

ANSWER: Both show comparable recovery rates depending on the population they serve. There are special advantages for outpatient treatment that include being able to continue working, living at home, and developing peer relationships with other recovering alcoholics who live in the community and with whom one will attend neighborhood A.A. meetings. Another advantage to outpatient care is that the cost is substantially less than that of inpatient treatment.

However, there are equally significant advantages to inpatient treatment, including twenty-four-hour peer group living and involvement, the safety of supervised medical detoxification for those whose withdrawal symptoms are too dangerous to treat on an outpatient basis, and the therapeutically intensive environment of a steady schedule of counseling, group therapy, lectures, treatment assignments, physical exercise and conditioning, nutritional therapy (if needed), and the constant interaction with other inpatient peers. All the while there is medical monitoring.

People who do not require medical treatment for drug or alcohol withdrawal, who live in a stable environment with a helpful support system, and who are able to abstain from alcohol and drugs are most likely to succeed with outpatient care. Persons who have failed a time or two in an outpatient program, those who cannot abstain from alcohol or drugs outside of a treatment hospital or whose home and environment are conducive to drinking or drug use, and finally, those who are so seriously impaired from any illness as to require medical and other help to meet their daily needs are candidates for inpatient treatment. There are also a significant number of physically well alcoholic persons whose psychological state is disordered to the degree that inpatient treatment is highly recommended.

Both treatments have in common these elements: (1) physical, psychological, and disease severity assessment, (2) individual counseling, (3) group therapy, (4) lectures and reading assignments, (5) spiritual assessment and counseling, (6) physical conditioning, (7) nutritional counseling, (8) family therapy, (9) aftercare involvement, and (10) treatment philosophy based on the Twelve Steps of Alcoholics Anonymous.

QUESTION: What is aversion therapy?

ANSWER: Aversion therapy is a kind of conditioning based on coupling the sight, smell, and taste of alcohol with noxious or negative stimuli so that the person will want to avoid drinking altogether. One form of aversion therapy is called covert sensitization, which involves the use of verbal suggestion to associate imagined drinking with unpleasant experiences such as nausea. This form of therapy is used much less commonly than other forms of treatment.

QUESTION: Will you say something about acupuncture. I've heard that some people in treatment for alcoholism have benefited from it. How does acupuncture work?

ANSWER: Western medicine doesn't understand exactly how it works, but it seems to have some effect on the natural pain-relieving endorphin system in the brain and spinal cord. Acupuncture has been used for thousands of years in traditional Oriental medicine to relieve pain, and there are some documented reports about its effective use as an anesthetic for major surgical operations in China. In terms of relieving addiction, acupuncture has been used to reduce the withdrawal symptoms of heroin and other opium addictions with some reported success. There have been some attempts to treat alcoholism with insertion of the needles to a depth of 0.5 mm (millimeters) at three points in both ears ("lung," "shen men," and the "sympathetic point"). This procedure was done over a period of several weeks, both daily and at longer intervals. Results indicated that over a six-month period, some persons experienced a reduction in the number of drinking episodes. At the present time, it appears that the possible beneficial use of acupuncture would be limited to the treatment of opiate withdrawal. It is my opinion that it has no place in the treatment of alcoholism.

QUESTION: I am a health care insurance consultant. Are there any statistics to show that alcoholism treatment is cost effective?

ANSWER: Yes. A long-term study of over 3,500 identified alcoholics showed that following treatment, the total health care costs of treated alcoholics—including the cost of alcoholism treatment—declined from 55 percent to 23 percent from their highest pretreatment levels, whereas the costs for untreated identified alcoholics continued to rise. Another long-term study revealed that overall health care costs for treated alcoholics were 24 percent lower than comparable costs for untreated alcoholics. These studies provide evidence for the over-all cost-effectiveness of alcoholism treatment.

QUESTION: Are there programs available that do not base their philosophy on a "higher power" as A.A. does?

ANSWER: Yes, there is a program called Rational Recovery. According to the literature sent to me by this organization, Rational Recovery (RR) is a self-help program for people who want to break their dependency on alcohol or other drugs based on the principles of rational-emotive therapy (RET), a widely accepted and taught system of psychotherapy originated by Albert Ellis, Ph.D. Does RR require abstinence? "RR requires nothing from you; what you put in your body is a very personal decision. RR does, however, provide a potent strategy in Addictive Voice Recognition Training (AVRT) for achieving life-time abstinence from the offending substance. People in RR groups very often decide there is no place for alcohol or drugs in their lives. They learn that their use of these substances is an irrational choice. They empower themselves to rationally choose not to drink or use drugs—ever" (Ellis, A., McInerney, J.F., et al. *Rational-Emotive Therapy with Alcoholics and Substance Abusers.* New York: Pergamon Press, 1988).

There are hundreds of RR groups throughout the country and in many foreign countries, and a number of hospitals provide inpatient RR addiction treatment. To further quote from the RR literature: "The 12-step programs have been effective for many people, but many who have been in 12-step programs have not been helped. Many had trouble with the 'Higher Power' concept, others with dependency issues and life-time recovering. RR offers these people an alternative that is not spiritually based, but based on rational self-empowerment." Also, "there is no reason why Rational-Emotive Behavior Therapy cannot be used very effectively with people for whom spirituality is a central aspect of their lives" (Ellis, A., McInerney, J.F., et al. *Rational-Emotive Therapy with Alcoholics and Substance Abusers.* New York: Pergamon Press, 1988).

You can get more information about this program by writing to Rational Recovery Self-Help Network, Box 800, Lotus, California 95651, or by calling (916) 621-4374.

JAMES W. WEST

QUESTION: I read an article in *The New York Times* (May 27, 1995) about Moderation Management. What do you think about it?

ANSWER: There are DANGER signs and blinking red lights all over it! For the abstinent alcoholic who is searching for a way to once more control his drinking, this looks like a legitimate escape from total abstinence. If he is an alcoholic who, before sobering up through A.A. or other means, had a high tolerance for alcohol, lost control over his drinking, continued to drink in spite of adverse consequences, experienced severe withdrawal symptoms, and tried to quit many times without success, this program is not for him.

Proponents of Moderation Management believe that many who have been labeled "alcoholic" have a much less severe drinking problem and have found themselves in an abstinence program like A.A. at the direction of the courts because of a couple of drunken-driving arrests or as the result of some other drinking-related incident. There are two universities (Rutgers and Michigan) where studies and programs along the lines of controlled drinking are being developed. Possible candidates for these programs are given a comprehensive evaluation in an effort to eliminate and refer persons who are truly alcoholic. The differential diagnosis between the alcoholic and the nonalcoholic with a drinking problem is determined by considering whether one is an occasional alcohol abuser, with occasional trouble at home, at work, or with the law, or whether one is alcohol depen-

172

dent, with a high tolerance for alcohol, severe withdrawal symptoms, and loss of control over alcohol. Clearly, this has got to be a difficult sorting-out process because of the large middle ground where the signs for each kind of drinker merge.

For those who elect to practice Moderation Management, here is the format: total abstinence for the first thirty days; then, for men no more than four drinks on a single day and a limit of fourteen drinks in a week. For women, two drinks in one day is the limit, with no more than nine drinks in a week. There are already Moderation Management support groups in several cities.

You asked me what I think about this, and I have thought a lot about it. I believe that any person who has ever had a real drinking problem, no matter how mild, and who is abstinent and doing well risks losing all those benefits that come with maintaining sobriety for a very minimal gratification. In addition, the probability of progression to an irreversible major relapse is a reality. Dr. George Vaillant, a professor of psychiatry at Harvard Medical School and a leading authority on alcoholism, says, "Nobody [working] in the trenches is impressed with [controlled drinking]. Every time someone makes a good case, just wait ten years and you'll see they're wrong."

JAMES W. WEST

QUESTION: Are there different chemical dependency programs for different professions?

ANSWER: There are. The first movement to treat specific professionals occurred in the 1950s when a center was established to treat clergymen for alcoholism, and now there are a number of facilities that deal with problems unique to priests. In addition, about twenty years ago, the American Medical Association (AMA) and state medical societies set up programs to address alcoholism and drug addiction among physicians. Special programs designed to meet the needs of lawyers and judges quickly followed. Now there are programs for nurses, nuns, airline personnel, and law enforcement personnel. All of these have one thing in common: the goal of total abstinence.

A big advantage of these programs is that interventions by persons of the same profession are more effective, and follow-up among people of like professions is very helpful. The basic treatment for addictive disease is the same for all, but each group has unique differences in professional life that are addressed.

QUESTION: It seems that you *always* refer your alcoholic readers who need help to Alcoholics Anonymous. Why is it that you never mention other support groups that have a very high success rate, such as Rational Recovery and S.O.S., which as part of their therapy do not emphasize a reliance on a "higher power," which is so repugnant to many rational and enlightened individuals?

ANSWER: First, let me say that A.A. has a record of success for more than fifty years. For those persons reaching for recovery who don't seem to be able to participate in A.A. because the "higher power" concept proves to be an insurmountable barrier, there are alternative programs such as Rational Recovery (RR—a program based on the psychological principles of rational-emotive therapy developed by Dr. Albert Ellis), Women for Sobriety, and the Secular Organization for Sobriety (S.O.S.). Al Wright, Director of the Los Angeles County Office of Alcohol Programs, remarks that "there is no particular approach that works for everyone—and . . . there is just about no approach that doesn't work for someone."

QUESTION: I have been shooting heroin for a long time. I haven't missed work and most people don't know I'm doing this or I would lose my job. I am able to kick it for a couple of months but I go back. Is there someplace I could go for treatment that wouldn't cost too much so that I could keep working? I don't want to go on methadone.

175

Answer: Pick up the phone, right now, and repeat the question you sent to me. The number is (818) 773-9999 (English and Spanish). Narcotics Anonymous (N.A.) treatment is confidential, anonymous, free, effective, available—and they're waiting for you.

Question: I have been going to A.A. meetings for about two years and I have heard it all. I am moving to a new city, and I'm inclined not to start these meetings again when I relocate. What is your experience with people who follow this plan?

Answer: I have probably detoxified a number of them without knowing this was the plan that resulted in their relapse. Remember, it is the nature of the illness that one is more vulnerable in times of change so I would strongly advise that you get to meetings immediately upon your arrival in your new location. Your plan may be an unrecognized emergence of denial. My guess is that there are still some things you haven't heard: that is, "You alone must do it, but you can't do it alone."

Question: Can you give me some idea of the recovery rates for people who have gone through a treatment program?

ANSWER: CATOR, a division of New Standards, Inc., evaluates outcomes of treatment and has a data base on over 65,000 patients from programs in thirty-five states. Overall, of those who complete a medically monitored intensive inpatient treatment program, 60 percent will have maintained abstinence at the end of one year, while 40 percent will have relapsed. For those with a lesser level of clinical severity who enter an intensive outpatient treatment program, 65 percent will have maintained abstinence at the one-year stage, whereas 35 percent will have relapsed during that first year following treatment.

QUESTION: Do alcoholics recover without having to go to A.A.?

ANSWER: Persons with alcohol problems (alcohol dependence or alcohol abuse) have stopped drinking without the A.A. program, and have done so for centuries. Professionals and others who know the disease see simply not drinking and recovery from alcoholism as two different things. There are those whose drinking problem ends with going on the wagon. These persons are dry, but for the most part are unchanged in their thinking and attitude. The lack of change distinguishes them from those who are dry and also in recovery.

Since drinking is only one symptom of alcoholism,

recovery means dealing with deeper and more resistant symptoms of the disease. These lie at the root of the illness, and their continued presence is the basis for relapse. Distorted thinking, most commonly manifested as denial, compulsion, dishonesty, fear, resentment, and selfishness, coupled with the syndrome of a low sense of one's own worth, isolation, low frustration tolerance, and oversensitivity, are the litany of symptoms that must be reduced or eliminated to reach the security and safety of recovery.

There are persons who have found recovery in a sudden rare kind of spontaneous conversion experience (William James: *The Varieties of Religious Experience*), and others who have found recovery in many different kinds of psychotherapy. All who recover have the common experience of a profound change in thinking and attitude about themselves and life in general.

The Alcoholics Anonymous program combines all the elements of effective therapy. One goes through A.A. in the company of other recovering alcoholics. Also, as with all other recoveries from emotional and mental illness, A.A. is based on a working spirituality. A.A. is accessible in every town and village in the United States and in every country in the world; it's free of charge, and best of all, it works.

QUESTION: I am a 51-year-old woman who has never exercised in a formal way. I have been going to A.A. regularly now for four and a half months and have not had a drink since then. I would like to start an exercise program now to get in better shape, but I don't want to go to one of those gyms. My doctor says I'm healthy now that I've given up drinking. Can you tell me how to go about this the right way?

ANSWER: Starting a regular exercise program can be one of the most valuable tools you can include in your recovery program. But I would suggest that you start by getting clearance from your doctor. Regular exercise is an excellent way to manage stress and anxiety as well as increase your feelings of well-being. It is important to develop a program that is rewarding and satisfying. If it's not fun, you won't do it.

Walking is a good way to start; begin at an appropriate level and set a regular time. Keep a journal of your progress. Warm up and cool down. Slow gentle stretching, focusing on breathing and releasing tension, is a good way to cool down the body after exercising. When developing a personal fitness program, involvement with a group is beneficial. Enroll in a class and involve others in your program. There are three basic types of exercise designed to increase flexibility, strength, and endurance. A well-rounded program would include segments devoted to each kind; it would emphasize endurance, which is good for stress release, but would also increase strength and tone muscles. Set realistic exercise goals. Set limits for yourself. Since exercise is a lifelong project, you need to formulate goals that will prevent injuries. Remember that gradual improvement will enable you to achieve a level of conditioning that will enhance your life and decrease your stress level, and remain a great tool in your recovery process.

PREVENTION

It has been said that the best prevention is early intervention. If the progress of alcoholism can be stopped early in its course, then great individual suffering and family disruption can be avoided. National efforts at prevention of alcoholism include education at all levels, increased publicity, and the creative use of media sources. Such efforts have already influenced nicotine addiction in older smokers, although the message of nicotine's harmful effects are just beginning to impact teenage smokers. But alcohol and other drug prevention programs do have clear, positive effects, and prevention activities continue to be applied at local and national levels with different strategies for different target groups. However, as with most things, prevention starts with the individual.

Question: I heard that if a person follows a well-balanced diet, regular use of alcohol will cause little or no harm. True?

Answer: Not true. Assuming regular use of alcohol means daily consumption of 5 to 10 ounces or more, depending on a person's weight, alcohol inhibits the breakdown and absorption of nutrients by damaging the lining of the stomach and intestine, and impairs transport of nutrients into the blood. A kind of anemia is directly due to a deficiency of folates caused by alcohol. Likewise, nutritional deficiencies (specifically, that of thiamine, or vitamin B_1) have severe and permanent effects on brain function, so it is definitely not true that you can eat your way through nutritional deficiencies caused by alcohol.

Question: What is prevention of alcoholism? Does it work? I can't see any evidence of prevention being effective.

Answer: Prevention is the sum of all of our efforts to keep the many problems related to alcohol use and abuse from occurring. Efforts are becoming more effective and widespread, and here's how it works:

- Information dissemination—provides awareness and knowledge of the nature and extent of alcohol use and abuse;
- Prevention education—aims to effect social skills in making decisions, refusal skills, and judgment ability;
- Alternatives—provides for participation of targeted populations in activities that exclude alcohol and drug use by youth;
- Problem identification and referral—calls for identification and counseling for those youth who have indulged in age-inappropriate use of drugs and alcohol or who have indulged in their first use of illicit drugs;
- Community-based process—enhances the ability of the community to provide prevention and treatment services;
- Environmental approach—sets up or changes written community standards, codes, and attitudes about alcohol and drugs, including laws to restrict availability and access to alcohol.

This rather long answer to your question must include a response to your comment that you don't see any evidence of alcohol prevention being effective. In 1979 nearly 20 percent of all adolescents age 12 to 17 were drinking alcohol regularly. By 1991 that number had changed to 10 percent. The incidence of liver cirrhosis has also dropped significantly, and alcohol-related fatalities decreased by 10 percent, representing large numbers of young lives saved.

QUESTION: What is being done to prevent alcoholism?

ANSWER: Much research is going on regarding this very complicated disease. In the area of prevention, scientists from the National Institute of Drug Abuse are considering both the resiliency of the child against alcohol and drug abuse, and the risk to a child for drug abuse. Three areas are being targeted for research: family functioning and parenting, early problematic childhood characteristics, and psychological skill enhancement.

Families in which there is ongoing dysfunction and instability not only put the child at risk for drug abuse, but also lack the positive characteristics and influences that would enhance resilience to drug abuse. Effective prevention would direct a family's efforts toward mitigating problems and building family strengths.

A risk factor for the child takes the form of early conduct disorders and in some children, evidence of depression. Prevention of eventual drug and alcohol abuse in these kinds of children must include helping them intellectually in the areas of goal setting, analyzing and solving problems, dealing with strong negative feelings, and recognizing and controlling impulses.

Finally, and ideally, the child would be integrated into an environment of positive reinforcement where he or she learns social skills with peers. Research has shown that the lack of these skills may not be the direct cause for addiction, but that without the skills the development of drug and alcohol dependence is almost inevitable in the genetically susceptible.

QUESTION: Is there some kind of medicine that will work to prevent cocaine from producing euphoric effects in the way that naltrexone blocks the effect of heroin?

ANSWER: Researchers are getting closer to just such a drug. It has been found that the prime receptor in the brain involved in cocaine use is the D2, or dopamine, receptor. In order to make a drug effective as a blocking agent, it is necessary to identify a drug that has a greater affinity to this receptor than dopamine. The D2 receptor for dopamine is located at the base of the brain on the outer surface of a structure called the nucleus accumbens, from which most of the dopamine is generated when cocaine is used. Dopamine is called the reward or pleasure neurotransmitter, and its effect as it binds with the D2 receptor is the extreme high and exhilaration that the cocaine user experiences. This process would not be a cure for cocaine addiction but would render its use ineffective, and thus act as a deterrent to its use, while the deeper issues of addiction are addressed in a treatment program.

QUESTION: Is there any evidence that a prevention program of some kind has an effect on drug use with kids? It seems that it's almost expected that young people will use something in the way of drugs, and if not drugs, then almost certainly alcohol.

ANSWER: First, there are lots of kids who don't use any drugs, including alcohol—and they probably constitute the majority. But because such a significant minority of young people do use, or at least try, drugs and/or alcohol, the idea of prevention is an important one.

A long-term randomized drug abuse prevention trial was done in 1992 in a white, middle-class population by a group from the Institute for Prevention Research, Cornell University Medical College (Botvin, G.J., Botvin, E.M. School-Based and Community-Based Prevention Approaches, in Lowinson, J.H., Ruiz, P., Millman, R.B., eds. *Substance Abuse: A Comprehensive Textbook*. Baltimore: Williams & Wilkins, 1992, pp. 910–927). The results of the study show significant reductions in both drug and polydrug use in those seventh, eighth, and ninth graders who were participants in the program compared to those students who were not in the prevention program. Specifically, there were 44 percent fewer drug users, and 66 percent fewer polydrug users (tobacco, alcohol, and marijuana). A report on the study in the *Journal of the American Medical Association* (273 [14], 1106, 1995) concludes: "Drug abuse prevention programs conducted during junior high school can produce meaningful and durable reductions in tobacco, alcohol and marijuana use if they (1) teach a combination of social resistance skills and general life skills; (2) are properly implemented; and (3) include at least two years of booster sessions.

QUESTION: Pressuring a person to go into treatment is the worst thing a person who is trying to help can do. I've been urging my sister-in-law to lay off as far as my brother's drinking is concerned. He's had a bad car accident and I think this will teach him a lesson. She still keeps crying around the place hoping that he will decide for her sake and the kids he'll go someplace for a treatment. Anyway, I heard that people who are forced into treatment don't get anything out of it.

ANSWER: Wrong! And it sounds like the one who should back away from that situation is you, unless you can be helpful by supporting the efforts of your sister-in-law to get that brother of yours into treatment before he kills someone with his automobile or abuses his wife or children. People who are not willing or ready to go into treatment have the same or even better chance of recovery than those who come voluntarily to treatment.

In the past two decades, intervention, wherein a person is motivated by others to enter treatment using emotional factors, threat of job loss, mandate by the court, or countless other pressures, is very effective. Those people, once in treatment, change their attitudes, and as insight develops into the depths of alcohol-related trouble, they often become active participants in their own treatment. Once it becomes clear to concerned people that a family member, employee, or friend is suffering from alcoholism, strategies, starting with strong suggestion and progressing all the way through a formal intervention, should be undertaken.

187

This kind of intervention is done with the direction of a professional interventionist. Such a person can be found by calling any treatment center. Some interventionists are listed in the phone book under addictionologist or alcohol interventionist.

RELAPSE

QUESTION: My husband has been in A.A. and dry for six and a half years. Lately he has started to drink so-called nonalcoholic beer with dinner and occasionally at other times. I've told him that I'm concerned about this, but he insists that there is so little alcohol in this beer that it is safe for him. Your opinion?

ANSWER: This is one of the most frequent questions I receive, and my opinion is still the same: Alcoholics drink alcoholic beverages for effect. Although some alcoholics enjoy the taste of these beverages, it is not because of the taste that an alcoholic will drink to the extent that his or her life may be ruined. Nonalcoholic beverages do provide the taste without sufficient alcohol to effect a change in mood. However, 0.5 percent

189

alcohol by volume or slightly less is present in these beers and wines.

I've spoken to many recovering alcoholics about their attitude toward these beverages and, with few exceptions, they state emphatically that drinking them would be a distinct compromise to the commitment to sobriety. Others say that it would mean that "my mind is still on drinking." Still others suggest that they would "feel guilty and uncomfortable since the very taste of beer or wine opens up a past which is marked by remorse for me and pain to others." Some have told me that when they were served nonalcoholic wine it activated a craving for the "real stuff" that frightened them. One said he "felt like I was on the slippery slope to relapse," so that he ended his experimentation with these nonalcoholic drinks. A few recovering alcoholics told about having nonalcoholic wine with dinner occasionally without guilt or adverse consequences. Several others drink nonalcoholic beer on occasion and enjoy it without seeming to harm their abstinence.

As mentioned, these nonalcoholic beers and wines contain 0.5 percent alcohol by volume or slightly less, and if five or six cans of beer or glasses of wine were consumed in an hour, a blood alcohol level of about 9 milligrams per 100 milliliters would result—not enough to produce a mood change, but possibly enough to induce physiological craving. There are no published data on the relationship between drinking these beverages and relapse. I agree with most recovering alcoholics I've talked with that drinking them is a compromise that may put sobriety at risk.

QUESTION: My life has changed since I've become sober and I feel like I'm just beginning to live. I've become very interested in a man who I'm sure feels the same way about me. My sponsor says this can put my early sobriety (seven weeks) at risk. She says that relationships like this should be postponed until more emotional maturity sets in with longer and more secure sobriety on the program. She talks about me getting to know who I am and setting boundaries before becoming lost in some "romantic obsession." Does my sponsor know what she's talking about?

ANSWER: She does. Research about such a state of affairs was the subject of a dissertation ("The Prince Charming Syndrome," Judith A. West, Ph.D., 1983). In this original research, a large number of women were studied from the start of their sobriety; those who became emotionally involved with a man during the first three months of sobriety relapsed to alcohol or drug use at five times the rate of those who did not become involved in an emotional relationship of this type. Go slow in this area, and hold close to the A.A. group and your sponsor's wise counsel.

QUESTION: I am two months into recovery and I feel great. Although I don't have any craving for liquor, I continue to go to meetings. What should I look for that would send me back to drinking? (This will never happen again.)

ANSWER: I hear two things in your letter: The first is that everything is going along just fine and you feel that the drinking problem is "just about gone." On the other hand, I hear a note of anxiety that things may be too good to last. Your parenthetical statement that "this will never happen again" comes across more as a hope than a prediction.

Being on guard seems to be the right prescription and means you are going to any lengths to stay sober. It is clear that you have made a searching and fearless moral inventory of yourself and have probably found one or more of those four major parts of the alcoholic makeup: resentment, fear, selfishness, and dishonesty. Since these are not eradicated in a month or two, there is likely to be some work left on these.

Your craving for alcohol has been lifted and you feel great, so now it's time to remember that "alcohol is cunning, baffling, and powerful." One of the first things I would look for as a danger signal is a feeling of complacency, along with the idea that "all those meetings are not all that necessary, now that I have no desire for a drink." (Can you see the cunning of alcohol?)

Other things to identify are the beginnings of compromise of the truth (less than rigorous honesty); the reemergence of denial ("It wasn't all that bad"); the tendency to isolation (avoiding A.A. people); being critical and irritable and resentful; and, finally, wondering if you need A.A. meetings at all. Most persons in recovery have a joyous honeymoon period for a few months, sometimes longer, during which it is hoped that they will settle in to living to the fullest the Twelve Steps of

192

the A.A. program. Some persons misinterpret this period with the conclusion that "this whole thing is easier than I thought, and staying dry is automatic." It isn't—one's recovery has to be attended to constantly. This is a serious task, but it should not be grim. A deep peace and much happiness, through thick and thin (and sometimes there's lots of thin), is always the result of working these (not easy) Twelve Steps to sobriety.

QUESTION: What do they mean when they say that after being sober for years, if you start drinking again, your drinking will take off as though you haven't been dry at all? In fact, some say that it is worse, like if you were drinking all those dry years too. I am not planning to try this but a couple of members in my A.A. group described this, and I just wanted to check it out. I also wonder if you could explain why this happens?

ANSWER: Your friends represent the profound wisdom of A.A. Over the years and with thousands and thousands of men and women in recovery, it has been observed that when the occasional person who, after many years of abstinence, relapses (A.A. language: "slips"), the mental and physical consequences are more severe than they ever were in the past. The biological explanation for this is not clearly understood, but the possible cause may be found in the brain. The brain may have been damaged during the previous history of excessive drinking, now is older, and has lost its tolerance to alcohol. Those delicate circuits involved in the functions of memory and thinking seem to respond much more sensitively to the toxic effects of alcohol. One fact that is indisputable, however, is that chronic alcohol consumption accelerates the aging process.

QUESTION: The other evening I attended a banquet at which the dessert was Cherries Jubilee. I am recovering from alcoholism, and even though they say that there is no alcohol in a dessert after it is burned off, I think it is too risky to try. Am I right?

ANSWER: You're right, and you didn't miss much anyway. Any dish like that requires some alcohol, usually brandy, to allow the maître d' to accomplish his flourishes and start the fireworks. After the poof of the blaze and the last little flames go out, there is almost certainly no measurable alcohol left and usually only the flavor of brandy remains. But if you have any uncomfortable feelings about this, then enjoy the jubilee part, but skip the cherries.

QUESTION: I have been going to A.A. for a number of years now but every couple of months I slip. I put together a year of continuous sobriety three years ago and felt so good about myself. I have a sponsor and I go to meetings. Am I going to be one of those people about whom they say "He could never make it"?

ANSWER: It would be a pity if that were true. Take heart—many others have gone through this same relapse history and have made it. I suggest that you read the beginning of Chapter 5 in the Big Book of A.A., which starts by saying that "Rarely have we seen a person fail who has thoroughly followed our path." The emphasis throughout this first paragraph is rigorous honesty. If, with courage and with total truth, you take the steps with absolutely no reservation, and eliminate those things from your life which, in good conscience, can't be reconciled with living the steps, you will stay sober. Also remember, "You alone must do it, but you can't do it alone!"

RECOVERY WISDOM

IT SEEMS THAT the disease of alcoholism afflicts the gifted as well as us lesser beings. Nobel laureates, great writers, creative artists, brilliant achievers, and extraordinary intellects are among those who suffer from alcoholism. Abraham Lincoln commented that alcoholism appeared to be more partial to those "whose heads and hearts will bear an advantageous comparison with those of any other class."

From sadness, isolation, and despair, many emerge through recovery to reach greater heights than if they had not fallen. Life in recovery is a mix of gratitude and serenity. People speak of an aura of wonderment as they experience an intense freedom from being sick in such an unpredictable, compulsive, and tragically self-destructive way. Life in recovery also brings loving and still hesitantly hopeful dear ones and friends back into reach. There is a humility that arises from the awareness of the depth of the illness from which recovered persons arise. There is deep thankfulness to those who stuck with them. Coping with the inevitable hard and even tragic times is part of the matrix of a strong recovery.

Eventually there comes that positive attitude so necessary to being a helper rather than a victim in a society to which one now truly belongs and functions effectively. Recovery is available for all on the simple condition that they have a sincere desire to stop drinking or using drugs, that they are open-minded to a set of basic principles, and that they are willing to go to any lengths to get better. There are no hopeless cases of addictive disease. Although much has been written about therapies based on one's own inner resources and strengths being sufficient for recovery, the vast majority of those who get well have found that in addition to what they found within themselves, they also discovered a source of power outside themselves that is fundamental to becoming wholly sane. This other, greater, power leads to the spiritual foundation of recovery, and shows how the principles of spirituality and mental health are the same.

RESOURCE LIST: ALCOHOL AND OTHER DRUGS

The following is a very limited list of key resources:

National Clearinghouse for Alcohol and Drug Information (NCADI) Center for Substance Abuse Prevention (CSAP)
P.O. Box 2345, Rockville, MD 20852
(301) 468-2600 or (800) 729-6686

National Council on Alcoholism and Drug Dependence (NCADD)
12 West 21st Street, New York, NY 10010
(212) 206-6770

Alcoholics Anonymous (A.A.)
General Services Office Board
P.O. Box 459, Grand Central Station, New York, NY 10163
(212) 870-3400

Alateen, Al-Anon Family Group Headquarters, Inc.
P.O. Box 862, Midtown Station, New York, NY
10018-0862
(800) 356-9996 or (212) 302-7240

Adult Children of Alcoholics
P.O. Box 3216, 2522 W. Sepulveda Boulevard, Suite
200, Torrance, CA 90505
(213) 534-1815

Cocaine Anonymous (C.A.)
World Service Office
3740 Overland Avenue, Suite G, Los Angeles, CA 90034
(800) 347-8998 or (213) 559-5833

Narcotics Anonymous (N.A.)
World Service Office
P.O. Box 9999, Van Nuys, CA 91409
(818) 780-3951

To learn more about

THE BETTY FORD CENTER

contact our website:
www.bettyfordcenter.com
or
for information regarding admission
call 1-800-854-9211

INDEX